1

AVENUES
English Skills

Lynne Gaetz

TEACHER'S ANNOTATED **EDITION**

PEARSON
Longman

5757 CYPIHOT STREET, SAINT-LAURENT (QUÉBEC) CANADA H4S 1R3
TELEPHONE: 1 800 263-3678 EXT. 232   FAX: 1 866 334-0448
infoesl@erpi.com   www.longman-esl.ca

Managing Editor
Sharnee Chait

Editor
Lucie Turcotte

Copy Editor
Mairi MacKinnon

Proofreader
Lynn-Marie Holland

Photo Research and Permissions
Marie-Chantal Masson

Art Director
Hélène Cousineau

Graphic Design Coordinator
Lyse LeBlanc

Book and Cover Design
Frédérique Bouvier

Book Layout
Interscript

Illustrations
Louise Catherine Bergeron

Cover Artwork
Pietro Adamo. *Citta Series*, 2008. Mixed media on canvas, 36 x 48 inches. Courtesy of Progressive Fine Art and Galerie Beauchamp. © 2011 Pietro Adamo.

© 2011 PEARSON Longman Published and distributed by
ÉDITIONS DU RENOUVEAU PÉDAGOGIQUE INC.

Registration of copyright – Bibliothèque et Archives nationales du Québec, 2011
Registration of copyright – Library and Archives Canada, 2011

Printed in Canada   3456789   II   15 14
ISBN 978-2-7613-3840-0   133840 ABCD   ENV94

Acknowledgements

I would like to express sincere thanks to
- Lucie Turcotte for her magnificent job of polishing this book;
- Sharnee Chait for her gentle prodding and valuable expertise;
- Julie Hough for her encouraging words, which helped ignite this project;
- Mairi MacKinnon, copy editor, and Lynn-Marie Holland, proofreader, for their careful work on the manuscript and proofs;
- Frédérique Bouvier and Interscript for the creative layout;
- My students at Collège Lionel-Groulx for their insightful feedback;
- Diego Pelaez for his valuable contributions to this manuscript and the Companion Website;
- Rebeka Pelaez for her optimistic attitude as she worked on the transcripts and tests;

I dedicate this to my husband Octavio, who provided me with emotional support and patiently put up with my long hours on the computer.

Credits

Chapter 1, p. 6 Audio text "Internal Clock" © Canadian Broadcasting Corporation. pp. 12–13 "Finding Solace in Chaos" by Warren Wooden reprinted with the permission of the author. p. 14 Video segment "Home Is in Every Moment" © Lonely Planet.

Chapter 2, pp. 25–26 "The Brain and Medical Mysteries" by Radha Chitale reprinted with the permission of ABC News. p. 27 Video segment "A Cure for Stuttering?" © ABC. pp. 28–29 "How Singing Improves Your Health" reprinted with the permission of *SixWise.com*.

Chapter 3, p. 38 Video segment "My Broken Guitar" © Canadian Broadcasting Corporation. pp. 39–40 "The Compulsive Shopper" reprinted with the permission of Rebeka Pelaez. p. 45 "Diamond Marketing" by Robin Edgerton reprinted with the permission of the author. p. 46 Video segment "Pook Toques" © Canadian Broadcasting Corporation.

Chapter 4, pp. 60, 61–62 "The Emotional Lives of Animals," adapted from *When Elephants Weep: The Emotional Lives of Animals* by Jeffrey Moussaieff Masson and Susan McCarthy, © 1995 by Jeffrey Masson and Susan McCarthy; used by permission of Delacorte Press, an imprint of The Random House Publishing Group, a division of Random House, Inc. p. 63 Video segment "Christian the Lion" © Global TV; excerpts from *Christian the Lion at World's End* (Bill Travers/Virginia McKenna/Born Free Foundation) used with the permission of the Born Free Foundation; the full documentary film about Christian the Lion can be purchased from *www.bornfree.org.uk* or *www.bornfreeusa.org*. p. 64 "Zoo Story" by Thomas French © St. Petersburg Times 2007, reprinted with permission.

Chapter 5, p. 79 Audio text "Traditions in Somalia," used with the permission of Mawlid Abdoul-Aziz. pp. 80–81 "Wedding Traditions" reprinted with the permission of Diego Pelaez Gaetz. p. 83 Video segment "Rethinking Bullfights" © Canadian Broadcasting Corporation.

Chapter 6, pp. 93–94 "Killing Monsters" by Gerard Jones © 2003 Gerard Jones, reprinted by permission of Basic Books, a member of the Perseus Books Group. pp. 96–97 "My Childhood in Somalia" reprinted with the permission of Mawlid Abdoul-Aziz. pp. 99–100 "China's Little Emperors" by Jan Wong reprinted with the permission of the author. p. 101 Video segment "Adoption" © Canadian Broadcasting Corporation.

Chapter 7, pp. 107–108 "A Lesson in Brave Parenting" by Bruce Barcott © 2010 reprinted with the permission of the author. p. 109 Video segment "Thrill Seekers" © ABC.

This book is printed on paper made in Québec from 100% post-consumer recycled materials, processed chlorine-free, certified Eco-Logo, and manufactured using biogas energy.

Preface

Avenues 1: English Skills is the first of a three-level series. Designed for high-beginner to low-intermediate students of English as a second language, *Avenues 1* is a comprehensive integrated skills book. As the author of the *Brass Tacks*, *Brass Ring*, and *Open* series, I have spent many years exploring what works in my classroom and developing material that will engage and inform students.

In *Avenues 1: English Skills*, seven chapters focus on contemporary themes that will challenge students. The Start-up activity in each chapter introduces students to the chapter's theme. Additionally, Vocabulary Boosts and online exercises help students develop a more varied vocabulary. Blog posts, excerpts from books and textbooks, magazine and newspaper articles, and the final short story expose students to a variety of ideas and writing styles. In the Take Action! section near the end of each chapter, there are additional writing and speaking prompts. Chapters end with revising and editing exercises that can help students improve their writing skills. At the end of the book, three writing workshops contain detailed information about the paragraph, the essay, and revising techniques.

Because question forms are difficult for students to master, every chapter contains question activities. Additionally, visual aids help students retain concepts. Scattered throughout the chapters, grammar tips remind students about key concepts.

Avenues 1: English Skills is accompanied by a new learning-centred website, the *Avenues 1: English Skills Companion Website Plus*. To provide maximum flexibility for teachers, every reading, watching, and listening activity in the skills book has two sets of different questions: 1) Textbook questions can be taken up in class; 2) Online questions can be assigned as homework or done in a classroom lab. The automated grading function allows students to check their results; using the grade tracker, you can conveniently monitor their progress and verify that homework was done. To help students do better in reading tests, including Benchmark and TESOL tests, the website contains a Reading Strategies section filled with practice exercises on vocabulary and main and supporting ideas. Furthermore, students can do some of the extra reading and listening exercises available online.

The Teacher Section of the Companion Website includes a variety of class-tested reading and listening tests, evaluation grids, additional speaking and writing prompts as well as transcripts for the audio and visual material.

Avenues 1: English Skills includes more material than necessary for a course of forty-five hours, allowing you to use different chapters when you've exhausted certain topics. Additionally, you can present chapters in whatever sequence you prefer.

Complementing the themes in this book with clear explanations and exercises is *Avenues 1: English Grammar*, which thoroughly covers the key notions presented in the grammar tips with clear explanations and exercises. If students have particular difficulties with a grammatical concept, they can try additional online exercises created for the *Avenues 1: English Grammar Companion Website Plus*.

Finally, I'm delighted with the decision to print my books on recycled paper.

Lynne Gaetz

Highlights

Warm-up activities provide a relevant introduction to each chapter's theme.

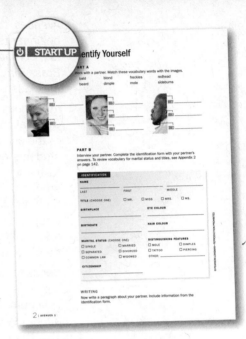

Effective strategies help students improve their reading skills. Online practice allows them to prepare for reading tests, including Benchmark and TESOL tests.

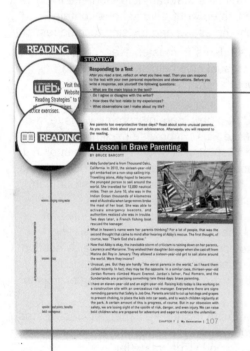

The *Avenues 1: English Skills Companion Website Plus* contains additional reading and listening material for further practice. It also includes vocabulary exercises and extra comprehension questions for all the reading and listening activities in the book.

Exercises and useful tips allow students to practise pronunciation.

Texts taken from a variety of sources expose students to different writing styles and ideas.

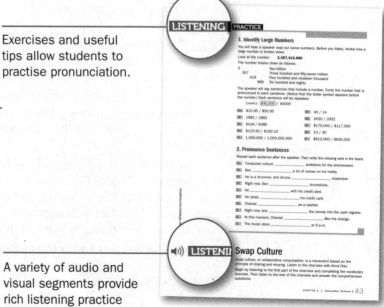

A variety of audio and visual segments provide rich listening practice material.

Vocabulary Boosts help students to build their vocabulary by examining the nuances between commonly confused words.

In each chapter, the Take Action! section includes additional writing and speaking topics as well as presentation tips.

Speaking activities particularly emphasize question formation.

The Revising and Editing section helps students to develop their writing skills and to prepare for writing tests, including the Benchmark and TESOL tests.

Throughout the book, Grammar Tips cover key concepts, which are further explored in *Avenues 1: English Grammar*.

- A Reading Supplement invites students to engage in a reading group activity based on a short story.
- Three Writing Workshops provide detailed explanations about the paragraph, the essay, and revising techniques.

Scope and Sequence

	READING	WRITING	LISTENING/WATCHING
CHAPTER 1: Self-Reflections	• Identify main idea and supporting details • Read: a textbook definition; a narrative blog; an online "how to" article	• Write: simple present sentences and questions (third-person singular) • Analyze character and motives • Write paragraphs • Edit a paragraph	• Listen: for pronouns; to phone messages; for main ideas • Listen to an interview about chronic illness • Watch a video about a man's reflections on home
CHAPTER 2: Mind-Body Health	• Identify cognates • Read online and news articles • Identify main and supporting ideas • Identify vocabulary in context	• Write: questions about health, lifestyle; a topic sentence • Brainstorm ideas • Practise using the simple present tense • Use question words in survey and interview questions • Edit a paragraph	• Listen: verbs ending in –s or –es • Listen to an interview about the common cold • Watch a video about a cure for stuttering
CHAPTER 3: Consumer Culture	• Recognize context clues • Identify main and supporting ideas • Read: an online article; a narrative blog; a magazine article • Do team reading	• Write: present progressive; past; questions • Write about consumer culture • Summarize main ideas • Write a paragraph • Use transitional words • Edit a paragraph	• Listen: large numbers; verb pronunciation • Listen to an interview about swap culture • Watch a video about consumer power; Dragon's Den
CHAPTER 4: Into the Wild	• Use a dictionary • Identify main and supporting ideas • Read: a narrative blog; a book excerpt; a newspaper article • Synthesize information • Do pair reading	• Write: present; past; modals; questions • Write about the natural world • Write for supporting details • Edit a paragraph	• Listen: for main ideas; to the pronunciation of past tense verbs • Listen to a debate about meat eating • Watch a video about Christian the Lion
CHAPTER 5: Travel and Cultural Traditions	• Identify the thesis and topic sentences • Read: online articles; a narrative blog; a personal letter • Do team reading	• Write: an introductory paragraph; questions and definitions; an opinion essay • Write about: travel, traditions, and sports; a partner's responses • Edit an essay	• Listen: for main ideas and details; to details about prices, dates, and places; to directions • Listen to an interview about Somalia • Watch a video about bullfights
CHAPTER 6: The Early Years	• Identify the message • Read: two book excerpts; an interview • Do team reading • Identify main idea and understand details	• Write: questions and definitions; a conclusion • Dictation • Summarize information • Write about gender, the family, birth order, disciplining, and adoption • Edit an essay	• Listen: for main ideas and details; to the pronunciation of th • Listen to an interview about children and gender stereotyping • Watch a video about adoption • Watch a video about hyper-parenting (website)
CHAPTER 7: My Generation	• Respond to a text • Identify main ideas and understand details • Read: a newspaper article; an interview; a personal article • Identify the message	• Write: questions using all tenses; comparisons • Write about generations and subcultures • Support opinions • Revise for sentence variety • Edit for mixed errors	• Listen: to words containing silent letters; for main and supporting ideas • Identify word endings • Listen to an interview about the 1990s • Watch a video about thrill seekers
Reading Supplement	• Read a short story		

SPEAKING	VOCABULARY	GRAMMAR	REVISING AND EDITING
• Make introductions • Share information • Interview a partner • Pronounce: pronouns; sentences • Presentation topics	• Learn: personal identification terms; new verbs related to habits • Vocabulary Boosts: *alone, lonely,* and *only*; telling the time	• Form questions • Learn capitalization rules • Write birthdates • Practise using third-person singular subjects • Identify pronoun errors	• Revise a paragraph for adequate supporting details • Edit a paragraph for pronoun usage
• Practise using question words • Discuss common illnesses • Doctor-patient role play • Interview a partner • Conduct a survey • Pronounce: verbs ending in –s; sentences	• Learn medical vocabulary • Learn terms: *remember, memory,* and *souvenir* • Vocabulary Boost: *make, do, play,* and *go*	• Form questions and use question words • Practise: subject-verb agreement; using the present and past tenses • Use adjectives • Identify errors in present tense verbs	• Revise a paragraph for the main idea (add a topic sentence) • Edit a paragraph for present tense verbs
• Interview a partner about: spending habits; past and current trends • Form questions • Present past, present, and future trends	• Describe clothing and consumer environments • Vocabulary Boosts: *for sale, on sale,* and *sell; win* and *earn* • Identify numbers	• Use the present progressive in comparisons • Use: adjectives; present and future verbs • Form questions • Identify errors in progressive verbs	• Revise for transitional expressions • Edit for present progressive verbs
• Discuss: nature; ethics and animals • Pronounce: past tense verbs; sentences • Ask questions using various tenses and *would*	• Learn vocabulary about nature • Vocabulary Boost: *woods* and *nature* • Describe objects • Define words	• Form past tense questions • Identify past verbs • Use: *would*; adjectives • View verbs in context • Identify errors in past tense verbs	• Revise for supporting details • Edit past tense verbs
• Name countries • Interview a partner about: travel experiences; holidays and celebrations • Ask questions in a variety of tenses • Discuss sports	• Learn about: countries and nationalities; the names of holidays and celebrations; gestures; directions vocabulary • Vocabulary Boost: travel terms • Define words	• Form questions • Use: *the; should; will*; adjectives • Identify errors in modals and verbs • Practise present, past, and future tenses	• Revise for an introduction • Edit an essay for modal forms
• Discuss gender stereotypes • Interview a partner about childhood and gender stereotypes • Pronounce *t* and *th* • Describe a role model • Discuss birth order	• Use: action verbs; comparative forms of adjectives • Learn: family member names; vocabulary related to adoption	• Use modals • Form questions • Give advice • Practice past, present, and future tenses • Make comparisons • Identify errors in plural forms	• Revise for a conclusion • Edit an essay for singular and plural forms
• Discuss: lifestyles in the past; subcultures; your generation • Present parenting rules • Present problems in society • Create a public service announcement	• Use: descriptive vocabulary; comparative forms of adjectives • Vocabulary Boosts: *let* and *leave*; past and present fashions	• Use: different verb tenses; modals; personal pronouns • Ask and answer questions • Make comparisons • Form questions	• Revise for sentence variety • Edit for mixed errors

Table of Contents

*"How you treat others is
a direct reflection of
how you feel about yourself."*

– AMBER DECKERS, WRITER

CHAPTER 1

Self-Reflections

What do you want to accomplish in life?
In this introductory chapter, you will have
the opportunity to write about yourself.

Identify Yourself

PART A

Work with a partner. Match these vocabulary words with the images.

bald	blond	freckles	redhead
beard	dimple	mole	sideburns

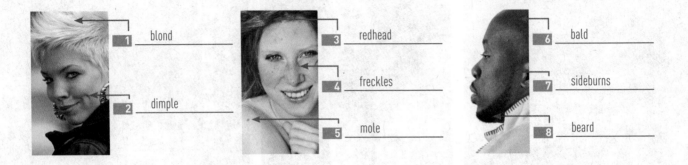

1 — blond
2 — dimple

3 — redhead
4 — freckles
5 — mole

6 — bald
7 — sideburns
8 — beard

You can present the chapters in whatever order you want. Chapters 1 and 2 focus mainly on the present tenses. In the Teacher Section of the Companion Website and in the "Take Action!" section at the end of the chapters, you will find writing prompts for all chapters that require the present, past, and future tenses.

PART B

Interview your partner. Complete the identification form with your partner's answers. To review vocabulary for marital status and titles, see Appendix 2 on page 142.

IDENTIFICATION

NAME

_____ _____ _____
LAST   FIRST   MIDDLE

TITLE (CHOOSE ONE)   ☐ MR.   ☐ MISS   ☐ MRS.   ☐ MS.

BIRTHPLACE   **EYE COLOUR**

_____   _____

BIRTHDATE   **HAIR COLOUR**

_____   _____

MARITAL STATUS (CHOOSE ONE)   **DISTINGUISHING FEATURES**

☐ SINGLE   ☐ MARRIED   ☐ MOLE   ☐ DIMPLES

☐ SEPARATED   ☐ DIVORCED   ☐ TATTOO   ☐ PIERCING

☐ COMMON LAW ☐ WIDOWED   OTHER: _____

CITIZENSHIP

_____

If you have time, ask students to introduce their partners to other students.

WRITING

Now write a paragraph about your partner. Include information from the identification form.

Grammar TIP

Age, Birthplace, and Birthdate

Age

Use *be* to state your age. Do not use *have*.

> How old **are** you?
>
> I **am** seventeen years old, and my brother **is** twenty. (I ~~have~~ twenty.)

Birthplace

Describe where you were born using the past tense of *be* + *born*.

> I **was born** in Halifax.   Where **were** you **born**?

Birthdate

Use *on* + month + day. Capitalize the month.

> Jeff's birthday is **on March 21**.

For more information about prepositions, see Unit 8 in *Avenues 1: English Grammar*.

Visit the Companion Website for practice in pronouncing and identifying names, ages, and birthdates.

READING STRATEGY

You can prepare for your reading tests by visiting the Companion Website. Click on "Reading Strategies" to find a variety of practice exercises.

Identifying the Main Idea

When you read, identify the **main idea**, which is the principal message of a text. It may be expressed in the title, introduction, or conclusion.

Sometimes writers do not express the main point directly. If you cannot find a statement with the main idea, then ask yourself *who, what, when, where, why,* and *how* questions. In a sentence or two, you can write your own statement of main idea.

Students can visit the Companion Website to practise reading strategies. Exercises on context clues, main idea, etc., are structured to help students do better in their reading tests, including Benchmark and TESOL tests.

There are extra questions for all of the readings in this book on the Companion Website. Created to give you maximum flexibility, the website questions can be assigned as homework or done in a classroom lab. Using the grade tracker, you can check students' scores and ensure that homework was done.

PRACTICE

Read the following excerpt, and then answer the questions.

Exactly when adulthood begins is not always easy to determine. For some, adulthood can be considered the period of life from the early twenties until old age and death. But in other cultures, adulthood is reached soon after puberty. Some people feel that it begins after graduation from high school, whereas others would say adulthood doesn't begin until after graduation from college. Perhaps adulthood is the point when a person becomes totally self-sufficient with a job and a home separate from his or her parents. In that case, some people are not adults until their late thirties.

Source: Cicarelli, Saundra K. *Psychology.* Upper Saddle River: Pearson, 2009. 342. Print.

1 Underline one sentence in the paragraph that shows the main idea.

2 List some supporting ideas.

> An age from the twenties on
>
> After graduation
>
> When someone is self-sufficient

In the following text, a young man argues that he is an adult. Read the essay and see if you agree with his assessment.

The Truth about Zac

1 My name is Zachary, but people in my family call me Zac.

I am twenty-four years old, and I live with my parents. It's great because I don't have to pay rent.

I go to university, and I study in psychology. I am also a father. My daughter Liza is five
5 years old. Liza lives with my ex-girlfriend, but Liza lives with me on weekends.

I work on Saturdays and Sundays in the stockroom of a large store. When new merchandise arrives, I move the boxes with a forklift and place them on shelves. I work nights, but that is okay because I am a night owl. I like to stay up all night and sleep until noon.

10 Often, my parents take care of my daughter because I am too busy. They love her, so they don't mind.

When I am able to, I give some money to my ex-girlfriend. I buy clothing and gifts for my daughter. My ex-girlfriend complains that I don't help enough, but I have many expenses.

15 My car payments are over $200 a month. I also have to pay for gas and for my university tuition.

I believe that I am a responsible and mature adult.

(202 words)

You might ask students to read "The Truth about Zac" aloud. They can begin to learn vocabulary from context. Ask them to deduce the meanings of *stockroom*, *night owl*, *don't mind*, *expenses*, and *tuition*.

Place students in groups of four and ask them to do the writing activity. First, they should debate whether Zac is or is not an adult. Each group should try to create a consensus. Then students should compose the six sentences and three questions.

After doing this writing activity in class, you can ask students to write a paragraph about adulthood as homework. (See the Take Action! section. The first topic requires students to use third-person singular forms.)

VOCABULARY AND COMPREHENSION

Answer the following questions.

1. What is Zachary's nickname? __Zac__

2. Who does Zac live with?   ⓐ His parents   b. His girlfriend   c. Nobody

3. How old was Zac when he became a father? __Nineteen__

4. What is the name of Zac's daughter? __Liza__

5. Who does Liza live with? __Her mother__

6. How often does Zac see his daughter? __Every weekend__

7. What are Zac's expenses? __Car, tuition, gifts for his daughter__

8. What is a stockroom? __A place where stores keep merchandise__

9. What is a night owl? __Someone who stays up late__

10. On weekends, who takes care of Zac's daughter?
    __Zac and his parents__

WRITING

Work alone or with a partner. Zac says that he is a responsible and mature adult. Do you agree that Zac is an adult? Give your opinion. Write six sentences to support your point of view. Also write three questions for Zac.

EXAMPLE: *Zac is not an adult. Zac doesn't live alone. He lives with his parents.*

COMPANION web+ Answer additional reading and listening questions. You can also access audio and video clips online.

Third-Person Singular Subjects

When you describe another person's habits, remember to put an –s or –es at the end of each verb. Add *does not* to negative forms.

He **lives** with his parents.   He **does not live** with his girlfriend.

To learn more about the simple present, see Unit 2 in *Avenues 1: English Grammar*.

◀)) LISTENING PRACTICE

The listening segments are included in the Companion Website. You can assign the listening activities in class or give them as homework.

1. Pronounce Pronouns

Repeat each sentence after the speaker. Then fill in the missing pronoun or possessive adjective.

EXAMPLE: *Karen found <u>her</u> wallet.*

1 Karen often loses _____her_____ purse.

2 Today, she doesn't know where _____her_____ keys are.

3 Her husband has _____his_____ own bad habits.

4 Mr. Henry Hall always bites _____his_____ pens and pencils.

5 At work, he often sings when _____he_____ is bored.

6 His colleagues sometimes laugh at _____him_____.

7 Henry and Karen don't spend time with _____their_____ children.

8 They rarely take care of _____themselves_____.

9 My brother and I sometimes lie to _____our_____ parents.

10 What are _____your_____ bad habits?

2. Take Telephone Messages

You will hear two telephone conversations. Complete the information in each memo.

CALL 1

DOCTOR'S APPOINTMENT

NAME: _____Anjelica Benjori_____

MEDICARE NUMBER: _____BENA 2402 5112_____

DATE OF APPOINTMENT: _____Tuesday November 12_____

TIME OF APPOINTMENT: _____Noon_____

REASON FOR APPOINTMENT: _____Yearly checkup_____

CALL 2

JOB APPLICATION

NAME (UNDERLINE ONE): MR./MISS/MRS./<u>MS.</u>

FIRST NAME: _____Jeanie_____

INITIAL: __G.__ LAST NAME: _____Jericho_____

MARITAL STATUS (CHOOSE ONE):
☑ SINGLE ☐ MARRIED ☐ COMMON LAW ☐ WIDOWED

BIRTHDATE: February 23, _____1991_____

STREET ADDRESS: _____1463_____ Rice Avenue

CITY: _____Calgary_____, Alberta POSTAL CODE: _____T2K 4G8_____

PHONE NUMBER: _____(403) 655-1813_____

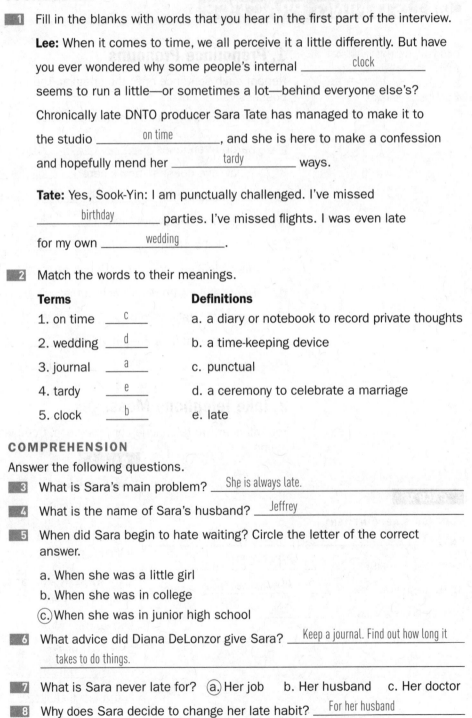

🔊 **LISTENING** Internal Clock

Your internal clock determines when you sleep and wake up. It also influences how you perceive time. Do you make others wait? Are you always late or always early for events? Sook-Yin Lee interviews Sara Tate about her chronic lateness.

Begin by listening to the first part of the interview and completing the vocabulary exercise. Then listen to the rest of the interview and answer the comprehension questions.

VOCABULARY

1 Fill in the blanks with words that you hear in the first part of the interview.

Lee: When it comes to time, we all perceive it a little differently. But have you ever wondered why some people's internal _____clock_____ seems to run a little—or sometimes a lot—behind everyone else's? Chronically late DNTO producer Sara Tate has managed to make it to the studio _____on time_____, and she is here to make a confession and hopefully mend her _____tardy_____ ways.

Tate: Yes, Sook-Yin: I am punctually challenged. I've missed _____birthday_____ parties. I've missed flights. I was even late for my own _____wedding_____.

2 Match the words to their meanings.

Terms	Definitions
1. on time ___c___	a. a diary or notebook to record private thoughts
2. wedding ___d___	b. a time-keeping device
3. journal ___a___	c. punctual
4. tardy ___e___	d. a ceremony to celebrate a marriage
5. clock ___b___	e. late

COMPREHENSION

Answer the following questions.

3 What is Sara's main problem? _She is always late._

4 What is the name of Sara's husband? _Jeffrey_

5 When did Sara begin to hate waiting? Circle the letter of the correct answer.

   a. When she was a little girl

   b. When she was in college

   (c.) When she was in junior high school

6 What advice did Diana DeLonzor give Sara? _Keep a journal. Find out how long it takes to do things._

7 What is Sara never late for? (a.) Her job   b. Her husband   c. Her doctor

8 Why does Sara decide to change her late habit? _For her husband_

© PEARSON LONGMAN • REPRODUCTION PROHIBITED

Are the next sentences true or false? Circle T for "true" or F for "false."

9 Sara's husband doesn't care that she is always late.　　T　　(F)

10 Diana DeLonzor wrote a book.　　(T)　　F

WRITING

Write a paragraph about lateness. Describe if you are a punctual person or a late person. Explain how you feel when you are waiting for someone. What is your opinion of people who are always late?

Telling the Time

With digital clocks and watches, people use precise numbers to tell the time. Use *a.m.* in the morning and *p.m.* in the afternoon and evening.

It is **9:36** a.m.

It is **5:21** p.m.

Use **o'clock** when it is exactly one o'clock, two o'clock, and so on. You cannot say "two fifteen o'clock." At 12:00 in the day, say "**noon**." At 12:00 in the night, say "**midnight**."

With regular clocks and watches, people tell the time using "minutes to the hour" or "minutes after the hour." Note that you don't have to say the word *minutes*.

to
It is 11:55.

past (or after)
It is 9:10.

It is five (minutes) **to** twelve.

It is ten (minutes) **past** (or **after**) nine.

Time can also be divided into quarters and halves.

It is a **quarter** to twelve.　　It is **half** past eight.　　It is a **quarter** after (or past) twelve.

PRACTICE

Write each time using *to* or *past*.

EXAMPLE: *2:40* _____*It is twenty to three.*_____

1 11:15 _____It is a quarter past eleven._____

2 6:30 _____It is half past six._____

3	7:10	It is ten past seven.
4	4:20	It is twenty past four.
5	9:50	It is ten to ten.
6	1:45	It is a quarter to two.
7	2:25	It is twenty-five minutes past two.
8	12:00	It is 12 o'clock. It is noon. It is midnight.

 For more practice telling the time, visit the Companion Website.

Go over the Reflections questions with students. After they write their paragraphs, you can ask students to exchange sheets. Then each student must write about his or her partner, changing *I* to *he* or *she*.

WRITING

Reflections

Write at least ten sentences about yourself entitled "The Truth about [your name]." Your paragraph should describe what type of person you are. Include photos or drawings. Provide answers to the following questions.

· What kind of person are you? Are you sociable or solitary?
· Do you have many responsibilities? What are they?
· Do you arrive for appointments or events late, early, or on time?
· Are you an early bird or a night owl? At which time of the day do you feel most active?
· Describe your living environment? Are you neat or messy?
· What are your passions?
· What do you value the most in your life?

Exchange Sheets

After you write your text, exchange sheets with a partner. Write down the first ten sentences from your partner's sheet, but change *I* to *he* or *she*. Remember to add –s or –es to verbs when the subject is third-person singular.

Vocabulary **BOOST**

Alone, Lonely, and *Only*

Alone means "by myself."

Lonely is an adjective that means "feeling solitary or isolated."

Only modifies other words. It can mean "the single one" or "just."

*Kendra lives **alone**. She is not **lonely**, because her dog is her companion. She has **only** one pet.*

PRACTICE

Fill in the blanks with *alone, only,* or *lonely.*

1. I travel _____ alone _____. I do not travel with anyone. I never feel _____ lonely _____ because I meet a lot of people in youth hostels. I am the _____ only _____ person in my family who travels.

2. Fernando is _____ only _____ sixteen, but he lives _____ alone _____. He doesn't like it. He often feels _____ lonely _____.

 **SPEAKING**

Compatibility: Finding the Ideal Roommate

Imagine that you live alone in a large apartment. You need a roommate. Ask three or four students the following questions. Write your partners' names in the spaces.

PARTNERS' NAMES: _____ _____ _____ _____

Are you clean
or messy?

Do you cook?

Do you smoke?

Do you drink
a lot of alcohol?

Do you prefer
to share food or
eat separately?

When do you
go to bed?

Are you more
sociable or solitary?

Do you pay your
bills on time?

WRITING

Write ten sentences. Explain whom you are compatible with. Also explain who is not compatible with you. Explain why.

EXAMPLE: *Sayid and I are compatible. He doesn't smoke, and I don't smoke.*

 **READING 1.2**

How does lying affect people? Read about lying and its impact on a man's life.

A Liar's Story

ANONYMOUS

If you cover this reading in class, ask a different student to read each paragraph aloud. Stop after each paragraph and ask students to guess the meanings of difficult words. For example, in paragraph 1, you can look at the words *forehead*, *payoff*, and the expression *was worth it*.

escalated: increased and got bigger

1 I remember my first planned lie. I was four years old, and I didn't want to go to daycare, so I pretended to be sick. I put a warm cloth on my forehead to make it appear that I had a fever. When my mother felt my head, my skin was warm. She lifted me in her arms and carried me to my bed. I felt a little guilty, but the payoff was worth it. I kept up the lie for several days until I got bored and wanted to see my friends.

2 My lies continued. As I got older, I lied to my teachers. I also lied to my friends. I told them fibs about my parents' jobs. I pretended to do exciting things. I even invented stories about my cultural heritage—with my brown skin I could pass for Latino, Middle Eastern, Italian, or Indian. My lies escalated over time.

3 These days, I lie about my age, my education, and my experience. I pretend to know things that I really don't know at all. In arguments, I say, "I saw it happen! It's true." But in my heart I know that it is a lie. Whenever anyone catches me, I justify it. "Everyone lies sometimes," I argue.

4 Last year, my buddy and I were discussing Italian women. To impress my friend, I invented a story about a trip to Italy where I met a beautiful woman named Lucia. A few weeks later, he asked me about the woman. I made a liar's mistake, and I mixed up the details. Shocked, he looked at me and said, "You're lying. It never happened." I protested that it was just a white lie. It was harmless. But my friend looked at me differently after that, and I could feel a change in our relationship.

5 Those close to me recognize my character flaw. My parents know about my dishonesty, and they bow their heads sadly when they catch me in another lie. Yet I am still very capable of fooling them. A few months ago, I lied to my parents when I totalled their car. My excuse was that a deer jumped in front of the car, and I swerved to avoid it. In fact, I was texting someone while driving. I was looking at my phone. I missed a turn and went into a ditch. I didn't want to look like an idiot, so I lied. Amazingly, they believed me.

6 My girlfriend loves me, yet I lie to her too. I tell her I'm at a friend's place when I'm really at a bar. I tell her that I'm at work when I really just want to stay home alone. I tell her that I love her when sometimes I am not sure. But the little lies are really starting to cause problems for me. About a month ago, she asked me to return a DVD to the store. I completely forgot to do it. Later, when she asked about it, I said that I had returned it. She saw the DVD in my backpack a few days later, and she was furious with me. She doesn't trust me now.

7 I know why I lie. I do it to get myself out of trouble. I want to look better, smarter, and more interesting than I really am. In the past, it made me feel smug when others believed me, but I don't feel that way anymore. My lying is a bad habit that I want to break. It is toxic to my relationships.

(604 words)

Students can read the essay in class or as homework. There are additional questions in the Student Section of the Companion Website. You can verify if students have read the essay by checking their scores with the grade tracker.

VOCABULARY AND COMPREHENSION

Answer the following questions.

1 In paragraph 2, what is a *fib*? (a.) A lie   b. A true story

2 What is a *white lie*? Check in paragraph 4 and make a guess.

A lie that does not hurt anybody

3 In paragraph 4, what is a *buddy*?   a. A child   (b.) A friend   c. A stranger

4 In paragraph 5, the writer says that he swerved because a deer jumped in front of his car. What is the meaning of *swerved*? Make a guess.

a. Drove quickly   b. Focused   (c.) Turned suddenly

5 When did the writer begin to lie? ___ When he was four years old

6 Who does he lie to?

a. His parents   b. His girlfriend   c. His friends   (d.) All of the answers

7 Why does he lie? ___ He lies to get out of trouble and to look better, smarter,

and more interesting.

8 Why does he want to stop lying? _His friends, family, and girlfriend no longer_
trust him.

Determine if the following sentences are true or false. Circle T for "true" and F for "false." If the sentence is false, write a true statement under it.

9 He did not meet a girl in Italy named Lucia.　　　　Ⓣ　　F

_____

10 He hit a deer on the highway and crashed his car.　　　T　　Ⓕ
He was texting someone when he crashed.

GRAMMAR LINK

11 **a)** Look at the first sentence in paragraph 6. Write down the two verbs in the sentence.

_____loves_____　　　　　_____lie_____

b) Why does *loves* end in *s*?
The subject is third person singular, so the verb needs an –s ending.

12 What is the negative form of *She trusts me*. See the last sentence in paragraph 6.
She doesn't trust me.

DISCUSSION

You could ask students to write a paragraph about one of the discussion topics.

1 What are white lies? Give examples of lies that people tell.

2 At the end of the essay, the anonymous writer calls lying a toxic habit. What are some other toxic habits? Give examples.

··· SPEAKING

Good and Bad Habits

Work with a partner. Ask your partner questions to find out about his or her habits. Indicate which habits your partner has or doesn't have.

Partner's name: _____

PERSONAL HABITS	NEVER	SOMETIMES	OFTEN
Do you ...			
· make people wait for you?	☐	☐	☐
· send a lot of text messages?	☐	☐	☐
· lie to others?	☐	☐	☐
· wash dishes after using them?	☐	☐	☐
· put items away after using them?	☐	☐	☐
· use facebook or other social networking sites?	☐	☐	☐
· read books for pleasure?	☐	☐	☐

HEALTH HABITS	NEVER	SOMETIMES	OFTEN
Do you ...			
· bite your nails?	☐	☐	☐
· smoke?	☐	☐	☐
· exercise or play a sport?	☐	☐	☐
· eat junk food from fast-food restaurants?	☐	☐	☐
· spend time in nature?	☐	☐	☐
· drive too fast?	☐	☐	☐
· go to bed really late?	☐	☐	☐

WRITING

Write two paragraphs.

1 In the first paragraph, write ten sentences about your good and bad habits. Mention things you do and don't do.

2 In the second paragraph, write ten sentences about your partner's habits. Describe things your partner does and doesn't do.

Grammar TIP

Present Tense Negative Form

In the present tense, when the main verb is *be*, add *not* to form the negative. For all other verbs, add *do* or *does* and *not* before the base form of the verb.

> **Be:**   I **am** <u>not</u> rebellious.   She **is** <u>not</u> lazy.
>
> **All other verbs:** I **do** <u>not</u> **use** drugs.   She **does** <u>not</u> **lie.**

To learn more about the simple present, see Unit 2 in *Avenues 1: English Grammar*.

 **READING 1.3**

Warren Wooden maintains a website, *TheHappySelf.com*. Read about how to find solace in a chaotic world.

GRAMMAR LINK

As you read, you will see some pronoun choices. Underline or highlight the appropriate pronoun. On the Companion Website, you can listen to this essay and check your answers.

Finding Solace in Chaos

BY WARREN WOODEN

1 Happiness can be elusive when life is too complicated. As daily commitments multiply, we shift between various tasks, create long "to-do" lists, and **juggle** complicated schedules. It's all part of making a living, but in the end it can stand in the way of making a life.

juggle: handle and organize

2 For most of us, true happiness consists of spending time with (<u>our</u> / your) loved ones and engaging in activities that reveal the richness and beauty of the world around (<u>us</u> / we / ours). We can't just walk away from our responsibilities, but we can find ways to simplify (us / <u>our</u> / ours) lives. Here are some ways to work toward a more peaceful state of mind.

3 **Question your dependence on material possessions.** Recognize the difference between the things you need and the things you want. Our culture bombards (<u>us</u> / we / our) with messages about material things that will make our lives better. The reality is that most of these things will **clutter** our lives. For example, Tim Roth had a high-powered job as a lawyer, but he was not happy with (<u>his</u> / her) life. Ultimately, he realized that possessions are not important for (her / <u>him</u> / his).

clutter: add chaos and disorder

4 **Think for yourself.** If you spend your life playing out a role that society or someone else defines, you're missing the chance to follow your own desires. Do not be limited by conformity. Why give up your freedom and allow all of your decisions to be defined by what you "should" do? Become a non-conformist and think for (ourselves / <u>yourself</u>). Let your passions be your guide.

5 **Create more free time.** Life is full of opportunities to earn money, give service, learn new skills, and make new friends. Some of us want it all. We fill up (<u>our</u> / ours) calendars with activities and obligations. We tell our friends that we have no time to spend with (theirs / <u>them</u>). But rushing from one activity to another leaves us with no time to slow down, observe, and let things happen.

6 **Prioritize your commitments.** Find ways to increase (<u>your</u> / yours) free time. Spend some time by (<u>yourself</u> / ourselves) and spend time with the people you care about most. Focus on calming activities. Shania West, for example, reduced (<u>her</u> / his / theirs) hours at work, and she chose to spend more time on (his / <u>her</u> / theirs) sculptures. She also spends more time with (his / <u>her</u> / theirs) friends and family.

7 **Enjoy the simple pleasures.** How often do you prepare a healthy and delicious meal and then savour every bite of it? Instead of rushing through meals, barely tasting what (<u>your</u> / yours / you're) eating, take time to enjoy your food. Invest time in other simple pleasures—take a relaxing soak in a hot bath, walk in the sun, or bike through a nature preserve.

8 **Focus on the present moment.** Instead of looking to the future, learn to focus on the present moment. Enjoy what you are doing here and now. You can find serenity in even the most **mundane** task if you really give it (<u>your</u> / our / yours) attention and do it mindfully. Remember that simplicity is a process, not a destination.

(562 words)

mundane: ordinary; banal

Source: Wooden, Warren. *TheHappySelf.com*. Web.

Answers will vary.

Students can listen to this essay on the Companion Website and verify which pronouns are correct. Also, basic comprehension questions appear on the Companion Website. You can ask students to do the website questions, the textbook questions, or both.

MAIN IDEA

1 What is this article about? Write a sentence that sums up the main idea of the essay.

It discusses things people can do to have a more peaceful and fulfilling life.

SECONDARY IDEAS

2 Identify the supporting ideas. Put a check mark (✓) beside five items.

☑ Take pleasure in good meals and other simple actions.

☑ Focus on your needs, not on your possessions.

☐ Get advice from people in your field of study.

☑ Be an independent thinker and follow your own passions.

☑ Enjoy this moment, and stop worrying about the past or the future.

☐ Spend all of your money because tomorrow may never come.

☑ Try to have a balanced schedule and create time for yourself, your family, and your friends.

☐ When you have insomnia, take some medication.

GRAMMAR LINK

3 Paragraphs 3 to 8 begin with a command.
Who is the implied subject in those sentences?　　☐ we　☑ you　☐ they

4 What is the difference in meaning between *your*, *yours*, and *you're*? Give definitions or examples.

Your: _____ Refers to something you possess _____

Yours: _____ It belongs to you: it is yours. _____

You're: _____ You are _____

5 Paragraph 3 refers to *material possessions*. Paragraph 7 refers to *simple pleasures*. *Material* and *simple* do not end in –s. Explain why.

_____ Adjectives are never plural. _____

You can assign the *Home* video in class or as homework. Comprehension questions appear on the Companion Website. You can also assign the "written response" activity on this page.

Home

William Mitchell produced a video for Lonely Planet. He gives his personal definition of home. Watch the video and then answer the following questions on a separate sheet of paper.

WRITTEN RESPONSE

1 Write six questions that you would like to ask William.

2 Write a paragraph of about 75 words giving your own definition of home. What does *home* mean to you? Is it a particular place? What makes you feel at home?

Take Action!

On the Companion Website, you can find evaluation grids and additional speaking and writing topics.

WRITING TOPICS

Write about one of the following topics. For information about paragraph structure, see Writing Workshop I on page 127.

1 Adulthood

Define an adult. Give examples of two people that you know. Choose people who are in their late teens or twenties. Describe one person who is an adult and one person who is not an adult. Your text should be about ten sentences long.

EXAMPLE: *Eric is not an adult. He lives with his parents.*

2 Good and Bad Habits

Write two paragraphs. Explain how you and others behave at home and college.

Home Life: Consider routines at home. Who do you live with? Who does the cooking and cleaning? What are your good and bad habits? Then mention someone who lives with you. What are his or her good and bad habits?

College Life: Consider your habits and routines at college. What are your work and study habits? Do you do homework on time? Do you prepare for exams in advance? Also describe the study habits of a good friend.

3 Driving Habits / Cycling Habits

Write two paragraphs. In your first paragraph, describe your driving or cycling habits. If you drive, consider if you speed or tailgate. Do you drive with both hands on the wheel? Do you text and drive? If you use another type of transportation, such as a bicycle, discuss things you do and don't do. Do you stop at stop signs? Do you wear a helmet? Do you use hand signals? Do you take your hands off the handlebars?

In a second paragraph, describe the driving or cycling habits of someone you know.

SPEAKING TOPICS

Prepare a presentation about one of the following topics.

1 A Special Place

Where do you go when you feel stressed and you just want to relax? Think about a place that is very important to you. It could be a part of your home such as your bedroom, basement, or backyard. It could be a public place such as a park, restaurant, coffee shop, library, or dance club. It could also be a place where you go on vacation.

· Explain why the place is important to you.

· Describe how the place looks. Use *there is* and *there are* in your sentences.

· Explain what you usually do when you are in that place.

2 A Good Life

In the video *Home*, William Mitchell makes a very personal definition. He explains all of the things that represent "home" to him. Alone or with a partner, make a video about "a good life." Give examples of everyday moments that make life interesting and valuable.

SPEAKING PRESENTATION TIPS

· PRACTISE YOUR PRESENTATION and time yourself. You should speak for about two minutes (or for a length determined by your teacher).

· USE CUE CARDS. DO NOT READ! Put about fifteen keywords on your cue cards.

· BRING VISUAL SUPPORT, such as a picture, photograph, object, video, or PowerPoint slides.

· CLASSMATES WILL ASK YOU QUESTIONS about your presentation. You must also ask classmates about their presentations. Review how to form questions before your presentation day.

Revising and Editing

The Revising and Editing sections at the end of each chapter help your students prepare for writing tests, including Benchmark and TESOL tests. You can ask students to do the activities with a partner and share ideas.

REVISE FOR ADEQUATE SUPPORT

A good paragraph should include supporting ideas. Practise revising a student paragraph. First, read the paragraph. Then, add examples from your own life or the life of someone you know. Your examples will help make the paragraph more complete. (For more information about paragraph structure, see Writing Workshop 1 on pages 127–129.)

The internal clock is the rhythm we have in our lives. The internal clock can determine when we wake up or go to bed. For example, I _____

_____

_____

The internal clock can also determine our eating schedule. Everyday, I

_____

_____

Finally, the internal clock can influence how punctual we are. My friend

_____

_____

EDIT PRONOUN USAGE

Practise editing a student paragraph. Underline and correct six pronoun errors, not including the example.

My friend Sylvain has some very bad habits. He lives with ~~her~~ his mother in Laval. He never helps ~~she~~ her with the housework. When he finishes ~~is~~ his meals, he doesn't wash the dishes. Sylvain ~~he~~ is spoiled because his mother cleans the house by ~~himself~~ herself. She doesn't ask ~~his~~ her son to help. But Sylvain has some good qualities too. My friend ~~he~~ is a good driver. He respects the driving laws, and he drives safely.

His or Her

Use *his* to show that a male possesses something.
Use *her* to show that a female possesses something.

Jonathan spoke to **his** mother.

Isabel drives **her** son to daycare.

To learn more about pronouns, see Unit 1 in *Avenues 1: English Grammar*.

CHAPTER 2

"Stress is an ignorant state. It believes that everything is an emergency. Nothing is that important."

– NATHALIE GOLDBERG, WRITER

Mind-Body Health

How much stress do you have in your life? Do you work and study? Do you have time to relax? This chapter looks at healthy living.

START UP Lifestyle

PART A

Write the correct question word under the image. Choose words from the list below.

who   when   why   how far   how many

what   where   how often   how long   which

| 1 how many | 2 who | 3 how far | 4 when | 5 why |

Frequency:
- ☐ once
- ☐ twice
- ☐ daily
- ☐ weekly

| 6 how often | 7 how long | 8 what | 9 where | 10 which |

PART B

Write eight questions about health and lifestyle. Try to use a variety of question words. Then ask a partner your questions and write down his or her answers. Your questions could be on the following topics, or you can use your own ideas.

sleep   stress   food   dentist

work   exercise   relaxation   doctor

Ask students to compose the questions in teams of four or five. Then, students can pair up—perhaps in a language lab—and ask each other their questions.

EXAMPLE: *Question: How often do you exercise every week?*

Answer: Twice a week

Grammar TIP

Forming Questions

Ensure that your questions have the proper word order.

Question word	auxiliary	subject	verb	rest of sentence.
How often	**do**	you	visit	the doctor?

To learn more about question forms, see the verb tense units in *Avenues 1: English Grammar*.

1 Question: _____

Answer: _____

2 Question: _____

Answer: _____

3 Question: _____

Answer: _____

4 Question: _____

Answer: _____

5 Question: _____

Answer: _____

6 Question: _____

Answer: _____

7 Question: _____

Answer: _____

8 Question: _____

Answer: _____

WRITING

Write a paragraph about your partner's lifestyle.

Make, Do, Play, and Go

Make means "to construct, manufacture, or create."

Make a cake, a sculpture, a decision, lunch, a meal, a promise

Do means "to perform or accomplish." Also, you **do** an athletic activity.

Do exercise, gymnastics, aerobics, Tai Chi

Also **do** homework, the housework, the dishes, the cleaning, the ironing

Play means "to participate in a game or sport." You also play an instrument.

Play soccer, baseball, hockey, chess, the piano, the violin

Go + verb (*-ing* form) refers to a physical activity that you do alone.

Go running, skiing, swimming, snowboarding*

* Note: You can also use just the action verb: I run, ski, swim, and snowboard.

Point out that for "*go* + verb (*-ing* form)" constructions, it is also acceptable to say "I hike, I jog, and I ski." Mention the importance of being consistent in a sentence. For instance, they should not write "I go hiking, jogging, and ski."

PRACTICE

Fill in the blanks with *make, do, play,* or *go.*

1 I am very busy. I _____do_____ physical activities every day. On Mondays, I _____go_____ jogging. Every Tuesday, I _____play_____ soccer or I _____play_____ hockey. In the summer I _____go_____ hiking, and in the winter I _____go_____ skiing. I sometimes _____do_____ Tai Chi to relax. I also _____play_____ tennis when I find the time. Do you _____play_____ football or baseball?

2 At home, I live alone, so I _____do_____ the cooking and cleaning. I _____make_____ my own meals. I _____make_____ supper every night. Do you _____do_____ the cleaning? What activities do you _____do_____?

For more practice using *make, do, play,* and *go,* visit the Companion Website.

READING STRATEGY

Students can visit the Companion Website to practise. Exercises on context clues, main idea, etc., are structured to help students do better in their reading tests, including Benchmark and TESOL tests.

In the Reading Practice, draw attention to *sensible*, *pain*, *cry*, and *actually*. They are false cognates for French speakers.

WEB+ You can prepare for your reading tests by visiting the Companion Website. Click on "Reading Strategies" to find a variety of practice exercises.

Identifying Cognates (Word Twins)

Many languages share words that have the same linguistic root. Cognates—or *word twins*—are words that have a similar appearance and meaning in different languages.

EXAMPLE: *English: visit   French: visite   Spanish and Italian: visita*

False Cognates

Be careful, because some English words look similar to words in your language, but they have different meanings. For example, in English, *attend* means "go to" (*I attended the conference*). The French word *attendre* means "to wait."

PRACTICE

Read the following paragraph and underline words that look like words in your language.

> When a crisis happens and a person is in pain, what is a sensible way to react? Is it useful to cry and scream? Is it better to be stoic and show self-control?
>
> Many medical professionals now agree that there is a mind-body link. Depression and sadness can actually affect the immune system.

Fill in the chart below with five of the words that you underlined. Include at least two false cognates (words that look like words in your language but have different meanings).

	Spelling in English	Spelling in my language	The meaning SAME	DIFFERENT
1	_____	_____	☐	☐
2	_____	_____	☐	☐
3	_____	_____	☐	☐
4	_____	_____	☐	☐
5	_____	_____	☐	☐

 **READING 2.1**

What factors contribute to resilient behaviour? A university professor decided to find out.

PRE-READING ACTIVITY

Answer the following questions. Then read the essay.

1 When you get a low mark on a test, what do you tell yourself?

    a. I deserved it. I am a poor student and I can't do well in college.

    b. I probably didn't study enough. I'll do better next time.

    c. The test was too hard. It was not fair.

2 When you woke up this morning, what did you think about?

    a. How many days are left until the weekend?

    b. I have too many things to do.

    c. Here is another day. I'm going to enjoy it.

3 Look at the cartoon panel. Write what is going through the player's head. Write the first idea that comes to you.

Developing Resilience

collapse: fall apart; break down

1 Why do some people **collapse** under life stresses? Why do others survive traumatic circumstances such as severe illness, the death of loved ones, poverty, abuse, or war? Psychologists know that there is no single source of resilience. Instead, many factors come into play, including genetic predispositions, social skills, and self-esteem. But one character trait, above all others, seems to help people cope, and that is the ability to maintain an optimistic attitude. Optimistic thinking can alleviate depression, and it has clear physical health benefits.

overcome: surmount; triumph over

2 There are many examples of individuals who **overcome** tragic pasts. Both Maya Angelou and Oprah Winfrey were sexually abused and raised in poverty, yet Maya is a successful author and Oprah is one of the wealthiest talk show hosts in America. Holocaust survivor Gerda Weissmann Klein watched as soldiers took her parents away in June, 1942. Later, the Nazis captured her brother. Klein spent the rest of World War II in a concentration camp. In spite of the horrors that she witnessed, Klein and her husband say that their conversations are of hope and their language of optimism.

land mine: explosive device hidden underground

3 Jerry White lost his leg when a **land mine** exploded. According to White, "They say what doesn't kill you makes you stronger. It's not quite that simple. I believe you have to decide it will make you stronger."

outlook: point of view

4 Some researchers say that a positive **outlook** is more important than a realistic one. Optimists look at problems as a challenge. They do not focus on the past. They avoid self-recrimination and guilt. Instead, they face the facts. They focus on possible **outcomes**, and then move forward. They choose to believe that their lives have a purpose.

outcomes: results; effects

5 Because optimistic thinking has mental and physical health benefits, some researchers are training people to become optimists. Psychologist Andrew Shatte is the co-director of the Resiliency Project at the University of Pennsylvania. Shatte and a team of graduate students are teaching resilience to children. The key, Shatte says, is fighting depression.

6 In a pilot program, psychology students showed seventy children how to develop more optimistic thinking patterns. For twelve weeks, the children learned that there is a strong connection between how they think and how they feel. They also learned to tell the difference between **self-defeating** thinking and productive thinking. Children looked at their own fears and asked, "What is the worst that could happen?" They had to test their expectations and see if they were realistic. They also learned problem-solving skills.

self-defeating: not helpful; expecting to fail

7 According to Andrew Shatte, children learn optimistic thinking when they face challenges. For example, a researcher showed a cartoon to students. In the cartoon, a coach is pointing at a zero score and angrily looking at the players. Students had to write what the player is thinking. One child wrote, "We let the coach down. We're the worst team ever." Another wrote, "He's so mean! It's making me sad." But a ten-year-old, Bryce Marcus, exhibited positive thinking. He wrote "The coach can be mad. So what? We'll do better next time." The three students had different internal dialogues, which led to different emotional reactions.

8 A child who came from a dangerous inner-city neighbourhood was helped by the Penn Resiliency Program. Miguel believed that he would end up in a gang. He told the group, "What is the point in doing anything? It is just the way it is." In the program, Miguel had to "de-catastrophize" the situation. He changed his thinking and looked for other possible outcomes. The boy learned that he doesn't have to focus on the worst-case scenarios. He can focus his energy on things that he can control. He can change the way he thinks, and he can choose solutions.

9 So, the next time you feel extremely stressed or depressed, consider your reactions. Find a way to dispute your negative thoughts, and focus on what you can do to make the future better.

(646 words)

Sources: Aubrey, Allison. "Resilience Helps Kids Fight Depression." National Public Radio. 2010. Radio.
Adams, Valerie. "Can You Teach Resilience?" *WebMD Medical News*. Web.
White, Jerry. *I Will Not Be Broken: Five Steps to Overcoming a Life Crisis*. Survivor Corps. Web.
"Gerda Weissman Klein." Personal Histories. The United States Holocaust Museum. Web.

Students can read the essay in class or as homework. There are additional questions in the Student Section of the Companion Website. You can verify if students have read the essay by checking their scores with the grade tracker.

VOCABULARY AND COMPREHENSION

1 What does *alleviate* mean? Find the word in paragraph 1 and make a guess. (Circle the letter of the correct answer.)

a. increase; grow larger   (b.) reduce; diminish   c. happiness

2 What do Oprah Winfrey, Maya Angelou, and Gerda Weissmann Klein have in common?

a. They are all Holocaust survivors.

b. They are all on television.

(c.) They all survived traumatic events in the past.

3 In paragraph 3, what point does Jerry White make?

a. People become stronger after a difficult event.

(b.) People can make a conscious choice to be stronger after a difficult event.

c. Life is not simple, and bad things do not make you stronger.

4 What is Andrew Shatte's job?

a. teacher   b. student   (c.) psychologist

5 What is the main idea of paragraph 8?

a. Miguel is from a dangerous neighbourhood.

(b.) Miguel, a child from a poor neighbourhood, learned to change the way he thinks about his life.

c. People should be positive.

6 What is the main idea of this reading?

a. Andrew Shatte is a teacher of resilience.

(b.) People can become more resilient when they learn positive-thinking techniques.

c. Some people are optimists and others are pessimists.

GRAMMAR LINK

7 Fill in the blanks with the correct words from paragraph 1.

Why _____do_____ some people collapse under life stresses? Why

_____do_____ others survive traumatic circumstances such as severe

illness, the death of loved ones, poverty, abuse, or war? Psychologists

_____know_____ that there is no single source of resilience ... But one

character trait, above all others, _____seems_____ to help people cope ....

8 Why is there no –s on *know*? ___The subject is plural.___

Why does *seems* need the –s ending? ___The subject is third person singular.___

DISCUSSION

In paragraph 4, it says, "a positive outlook is more important than a realistic one." What does this mean? Think of situations where it is better to have a positive outlook than a realistic outlook.

SPEAKING

The World of Medicine

PART A: MEDICAL VOCABULARY

Familiarize yourself with some common medical terms. Working with a partner, match the photos with the correct terms from the following list. Two of the photos have two answers.

| cast | dizzy | medicine | stitches |
| crutches | pills | sprained ankle | wheelchair |

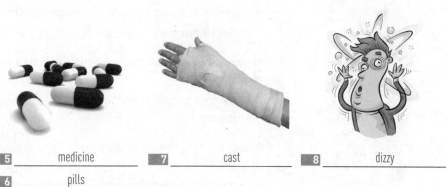

1 ___crutches___   **3** ___wheelchair___   **4** ___stitches___

2 ___sprained ankle___

5 ___medicine___   **7** ___cast___   **8** ___dizzy___

6 ___pills___

PART B: COMMON ILLNESSES

Write the name of each illness above the corresponding list of symptoms. Use your dictionary if necessary. Choose from the following illnesses.

chicken pox   measles   flu   cold

Illness	cold	flu	chicken pox	measles
Main symptoms	• coughing • sneezing	• fever • body aches • sore throat	• itchy red spots • fever • blisters	• skin rash • headache • fever

PART C: ROLE PLAYING

With a partner, role-play a medical scenario. Play the role of the doctor or patient, and just read the information about your role.

Patient Roles

1 You are coughing and sneezing. Ask the doctor for some antibiotics. Be very insistent. Your friend just got antibiotics for a cold.

2 You broke your right wrist. You do not want a cast on your arm because you need to keep writing with that arm. You have many important exams.

3 You are stressed and you want to have some time off work. Ask the doctor to give you time off work. You need a doctor's letter to show your boss.

Doctor Roles

1 Your patient has a common cold. The cold is caused by a virus. Antibiotics will not help. Do not prescribe antibiotics.

2 Tell the patient that you must put a cast on the arm. The patient cannot write with the arm or use it for one month.

3 The patient wants time off work, but there is nothing wrong with him or her. Do not sign any documents.

 **READING 2.2**

What happens when there are minor differences in brain wiring? Read about some medical mysteries.

PRE-READING VOCABULARY

Before you read the essay, review the meanings of the following words.

• *Remember* is a verb. It means "keep something in mind; not to forget."

  I **remember** the accident. It happened during a storm.

• *Memory* is a noun. It refers to the capacity to recall things or the recollection of past events.

  I have an accurate **memory**. The accident was horrible. It is a very bad **memory**.

• A *souvenir* is a memento that you buy or give as a reminder of a special place or event.

  I bought a **souvenir** in Banff. I bought a small Canadian flag.

Write one of these words in the blanks. Remember to add –s to the noun or verb, if needed.

remember   memory   souvenir

1 Alanis _____remembers_____ trivial details about the past. She has an amazing _____memory_____.

2 For example, many years ago, she visited Banff. Her friend bought a _____souvenir_____: a tiny plastic bear. Alanis _____remembers_____ many details about the bear. She has some great _____memories_____ of the trip.

The Brain and Medical Mysteries

BY RADHA CHITALE

Total Recall

etched: engraved; imprinted

1 For a few people, every moment they live is indelibly etched into memory. Wisconsin resident Brad Williams is one of those people. He can recall almost any news event and everything he experienced, including specific dates. "I am sort of a human Google for my family," the fifty-two-year-old told *Good Morning America*. In an experiment, Brad and someone with access to Google both received twenty trivia questions. Brad answered the questions eleven minutes faster than the person with a computer.

trivial: not important; insignificant

2 Another case is a woman who is simply known as "AJ." She revealed her condition to University of California brain researcher James McGaugh. Like Williams, AJ can answer obscure questions with mind-blowing accuracy. She remembers trivial details as clearly as major events. Asked what happened on Aug 16, 1977, she knows that Elvis Presley died, but she also knows that a California tax initiative passed on June 6 of the following year. And she knows that a plane crashed in Chicago on May 25, 1979. Some memories may have a personal meaning for her, but most do not.

feats: accomplishments

3 The condition is known among brain researchers as hyperthymesic syndrome, based on the Greek word thymesis for "remembering" and hyper, meaning "more than normal." While the brains of these people can perform amazing feats of memory, it is still not fully understood exactly how this occurs. One hypothesis is that their brains have different connections than the brains of most people. They are better able to organize and categorize information for later access.

Amnesia

4 Memory can also be extremely fragile. Perhaps no one knows this better than fifty-seven-year-old Beki Propst. Ten years ago, she experienced a grand mal seizure that robbed her of a lifetime of memories. "Everyone I knew before says my personality is the same," Propst told *ABCNews.com*. "But I don't know if I'm the same person." Details of Propst's case continue to confuse doctors. They know that a devastating "electrical storm" in her brain caused her declarative memory to be wiped clean. Facts, events, dates, acquaintances, and even her identity were wiped away. As Propst describes it, "If I were a computer, it would be like my hard drive was erased."

wiped clean: completely removed

5 A similar event occurred to seventeen-year-old Dana Kiger. During a routine soccer game, she fell and hit her head on the hard turf. The blow erased her memories. She no longer recognized her friends or family, and she could not recall who she was. Her brain had no physical trauma or swelling, so doctors were positive her memory would return. Yet, almost three years later, she still has no memory of her life before the injury. She says she is creating new memories. She focuses on the future, not the past.

Feel No Pain

6 In the *Millennium* series by Stieg Larsson, a major villain feels no pain. The condition is a real-life medical mystery. Do you think a life without pain sounds great? While pain is a sensation that very few of us enjoy, the absence of it can be tremendously hazardous. And for a young child, the inability to feel pain can be especially dangerous.

7 Eight-year-old Gabby Gingras recently learned that she has a rare condition. She does not feel pain. In an interview with *ABC News Primetime*, Gabby's father said, "I was massaging Gabby's gums one day, and she bit down on me extremely hard. When I pulled my finger out, I pulled a tooth out of her mouth—and she continued playing like nothing happened." Gabby's lack of pain sensation eventually led to the loss of all of her teeth. A badly scratched cornea forced doctors to remove her left eye, and she now wears a helmet and goggles every day to protect herself from serious injury.

8 As children with this condition get older, they face many hazards. They do not know if they break a leg or severely cut themselves, so they may not get medical attention when they need it.

(659 words)

Source: Adapted from Chitale, Radha. "Twelve Baffling Medical Conditions: Mystery Shrouds Some Conditions Despite Researchers' Efforts." *ABC News*. Web.

On the Companion Website, there are additional vocabulary and comprehension questions for "The Brain and Medical Mysteries." The online questions can serve as a practice test or as a formal reading test.

COMPREHENSION

1 Using your own words, explain the unusual conditions these people are suffering from.

Brad Williams and AJ: They remember everything that they learn or experience, including the most trivial details.

Beki Propst and Dana Kiger: They have amnesia. They have no memory of their past lives.

Gabby Gingras: She feels no pain.

2 Which condition is caused by brain trauma or an accident? Amnesia

3 Why is it dangerous to feel no pain? You can hurt yourself and not realize it.

Circle T for "true" or F for "false." Write a true sentence under any false statements.

4 James McGaugh can answer trivia questions easily. T **F**
He is a brain researcher. Brad Williams and AJ have that skill.

5 Beki Propst had a soccer accident. T **F**
She had a brain seizure. Dana Kiger had a soccer accident.

6 Dana Kiger was seventeen years old when she lost her memory. **T** F

7 Dana Kiger's memory returned three years after her injury.   T (F)

      She still has no memory of her life before the injury.

8 Gabby Gingras often hurts herself seriously because she
feels no pain.   (T)   F

RECOGNIZING COGNATES AND FALSE COGNATES

The essay contains some English-French cognates and false cognates. (See page 20 for definitions of those terms.)

Determine what the following words mean. Look at how they are used in the paragraph before you make your guess! Then decide if the word has the same meaning in English and French.

9 *Fragile* (paragraph 4) means

    (a.) delicate; easily damaged   b. difficult   c. not strong

    Does it have the same meaning in French?   ☑ Yes   ☐ No

10 *Hazard* (paragraph 8) means   a. guess   b. chance   (c.) danger

    Does it have the same meaning in French?   ☐ Yes   ☑ No

WATCHING

You can assign *A Cure for Stuttering* in class or as homework. On the Companion Website, students can watch the video and answer additional questions. You can check their scores with the grade tracker.

A Cure for Stuttering?

Stuttering is a speech disorder and a medical mystery. Watch the video and answer the questions that follow.

VOCABULARY AND COMPREHENSION

1 How old is Rebecca Glass? _Seventeen years old_

2 What does *stutter* mean?

    (a.) To involuntarily repeat sounds, especially the first consonants of words

    b. To stop and think

    c. To speak very slowly, carefully, and clearly

3 When did Rebecca Glass start to stutter? _In the second grade_

4 About what percentage of stutterers inherited the condition?

    a. 10 percent   (b.) 50 percent   c. 100 percent

5 What is Dr. Dennis Drayna's job?

    (a.) geneticist   b. speech therapist   c. psychologist

6 Which doctor had a stuttering problem as a child?

    a. Dr. Drayna   (b.) Dr. Kalinowski

7 What is the name of the earpiece that helps stutterers?

    a. No Stutter   b. Stop & Listen   (c.) SpeechEasy

8 How does Dr. Kalinowski's device help Rebecca?

    She hears her own voice repeated.

9 At the end of the segment, the host gives a warning. What does he say?

    (a.) The effect from the earpiece might not last.

    b. The earpiece can cause hearing problems.

    c. The earpiece is too expensive for most people.

If you love music, you might be surprised to learn that singing has health benefits.

GRAMMAR LINK

As you read, you will see some choices in parentheses. Underline or highlight the appropriate word. On the Companion Website, you can listen to this essay and check your answers.

How Singing Improves Your Health

enhance: improve

1 If you ever (has / <u>have</u>) the desire to break out into song—in the shower, in the car, maybe at your neighbour's infamous karaoke night—you should embrace it whole-heartedly. This ancient art not only (feel / <u>feels</u>) good, it can enhance your well-being, reduce your feelings of pain, and even prolong your life.

2 Using your voice to sing, rather than simply carry out a conversation, (offer / <u>offers</u>) unique benefits. "When we sing instead of speak, we have intonation, melody line, and crescendo, which gives us a broader vocabulary to express ourselves," says Suzanne Hanser, chair of the music therapy department at Berklee College of Music. "Because singing is visceral—relating to, or affecting, our bodies—it can't help but affect change."

chair: head; principal administrator

3 Studies link singing with a lower heart rate, decreased blood pressure, and reduced stress, according to Patricia Preston-Roberts, a music therapist. She (use / <u>uses</u>) song to help patients who suffer from a variety of psychological and physiological conditions.

4 Singing, particularly in a chorus, (seem / <u>seems</u>) to benefit the elderly particularly well. As part of a three-year study examining how singing affects the health of those fifty-five and older, a Senior Singers Chorale was formed by the Levine School of Music in Washington, D.C. The seniors involved in the chorale—as well as seniors involved in two separate arts groups involving writing and painting—showed significant health improvements compared to those in the control groups. Specifically, the arts groups reported thirty fewer doctors' visits, fewer eyesight problems, less incidence of depression, and less need for medication.

5 Even lead researcher Dr. Gene D. Cohen, director of the Center on Aging at George Washington University, was surprised at how big of (a / <u>an</u>) effect the seniors' arts participation had on their health. Cohen said, "The average age of all the subjects was eighty. This is higher than life expectancy. So, realistically, if an effect were to be achieved, one would ordinarily expect to see less decline in the intervention group compared to the control. The fact that there was so much improvement in many (area / <u>areas</u>) was the surprise factor."

6 The seniors also noticed health improvements, said Jeanne Kelly, director of the Levine School of Music, who led the choral group. The seniors report feeling better both in daily life and while singing. Their everyday voice quality is better. They (is / <u>are</u>) able to breathe more easily, and they have better posture.

7 The part of the brain that (work / <u>works</u>) with speech is different than the part that processes music. That allows people who can no longer converse to still enjoy music, said Clive Ballard, professor of age-related diseases at King's College,

London. "People seem to enjoy doing something jointly with other people. There (is / are) a lot of evidence that being socially engaged is good for people with dementia," Ballard added. Singing tutor Liz McNaughton says, "People who lost their ability to speak can access songs and words from the melody."

treatment tool: a method of helping patients

8 The arts are showing up as a **treatment tool** in hospitals across the country. In fact, a survey by the Society for the Arts in Healthcare found that 68 percent of the hospitals surveyed incorporated some form of arts therapy into their treatment option. And, if you are thinking of volunteering, singing at a hospital may be a good choice—not only for the patients, but also for you.

(561 words)

Source: "How Singing Improves Your Health (Even If Other People Shouldn't Hear You Singing)." *www.SixWise. com.* N.p., 7 June 2006. Web.

VOCABULARY AND COMPREHENSION

On the Companion Website, there are additional questions for "How Singing Improves Your Health." You can check students' scores with the grade tracker.

1 How is singing good for the health? List a few ways.

It can reduce pain, prolong life, lower heart rate, decrease blood pressure, and reduce stress.

2 Find a verb in paragraph 3 that means "connect." ___Link___

3 Who does *the elderly* refer to? See paragraph 4.

a. Children and young adults

(b.) Senior citizens (older men and women)

c. People in the medical profession

4 Paragraphs 4 and 5 mention a study. Indicate if the sentences are true (T) or false (F).

a. The study lasted for three years.   (T)   F

b. Only men participated in the study.   T   (F)

c. Some people in the study sang, and others wrote or painted.   (T)   F

d. The arts groups had health benefits.   (T)   F

e. The average age of the people in the study was fifty-five.   T   (F)

f. The lead researcher was Dr. Gene D. Cohen.   (T)   F

5 Why was Cohen surprised at the results of the study?

a. He expected the people in the arts group to do worse than the others.

(b.) The people in the arts group not only had less decline, but their health also improved greatly in many areas.

c. The study was not expensive.

6 In paragraph 8, what does *volunteering* mean? Look at the paragraph again and make a guess.

Volunteering means "working to help others, but for no money."

DISCUSSION

1 What role does music play in your life?

2 Do you sing alone or in front of people? Why or why not?

Conduct a Survey

You can do the survey in class. Divide students into teams to write their survey questions. When they finish, one student from each team remains in place and the others split up to join other groups in the class. In the newly formed groups, students take turns surveying the rest of the team members. The students then go back to their original teams and compile the results.

You might arrange for your students to survey English students in another class. Ask teams to peer-edit one another's surveys.

Work with a team and make up a survey about music, reading, writing, or art. Prepare five questions.

· Ensure that your questions have the correct word order!

· Give a choice of answers for each question.

> EXAMPLES: *Do you play a musical instrument?*   ☐ *Yes*   ☐ *No*
>
> *How often do you read a book?*
>
> a. *Never*   b. *Once a year*   c. *Every month*   d. *Every week*

· If you ask a knowledge question, give respondents an "I don't know" choice.

> EXAMPLE: *Who was Martha Graham?*
>
> a. *A painter*   b. *A dancer*   c. *An actress*   d. *I don't know*

After you have completed your questions, one of you will remain in place, and the rest will join other teams and survey the members. When the surveys are finished, go back to your original team to compile the results and present them to the class.

◀)) **LISTENING PRACTICE**

1. Pronounce –s Verb Endings

When present tense verbs follow a third-person singular subject, the verb ends in –s or –es. There are different ways to pronounce the final ending.

Pronunciation
TIP

Third Person Singular

Most verbs end in an –s or –z sound.

> EXAMPLES: *write   writes [s]*   *love   loves [z]*

Add –es to verbs ending in –s, –ch, –sh, –x, or –z. Pronounce the final –es as a separate syllable.

> EXAMPLES: *push   pushes [pushiz]*   *reach   reaches [reachiz]*

The listening segments are included in the Companion Website. You can assign the listening activities in class or give them as homework.

Pronounce each verb after the speaker. You will say each verb twice. Then indicate if the verb ends with an –s, a –z, or an –iz sound. Circle the correct choice.

1	hopes	(s)	z	iz	6	forces	s	z	(iz)
2	races	s	z	(iz)	7	feels	s	(z)	iz
3	watches	s	z	(iz)	8	teaches	s	z	(iz)
4	laughs	(s)	z	iz	9	kisses	s	z	(iz)
5	tries	s	(z)	iz	10	smiles	s	(z)	iz

2. Pronounce Sentences in the Simple Present

Repeat each sentence after the speaker. Then fill in the blanks with the words that you hear. You can use contracted forms.

> EXAMPLE: *Samuel _____talks_____ on his cellphone every day.*

1 Emily _____loves_____ to watch videos online.

2 She _____doesn't use_____ her television.

3 Many people _____don't pay_____ for DVDs.

4 Emily downloads movies and _____watches_____ them.

5 Samuel _____uses_____ his cellphone constantly.

6 Every day, he _____carries_____ his phone in his pocket.

7 Samuel _____doesn't have_____ a land-line telephone.

8 He _____doesn't make_____ long-distance calls.

9 They _____have_____ addictions to technology.

10 Emily _____doesn't know_____ how to live without a computer.

◀))) **LISTENING**

Please note that "The Common Cold" has different questions online.

The Common Cold

Is there a cure for the common cold? Listen and find out.

COMPREHENSION

1 Which illness damages cells?   a. a cold   (b.) a flu

2 Why do young people get more colds than older people?

Older people had many colds and developed the antibodies to fight them.

_____

3 How do most people get colds?

a. They stay outside in cold weather.

(b.) They touch a contaminated surface and then touch their faces.

c. The virus is in the air.

4 Is it a good idea to buy antibacterial soap to prevent a cold?   ☐Yes   ☑No

5 Why do more people get colds during the winter months?

People stay inside together and pass the cold to each other.

Determine if the following statements are true or false. Circle T for "true" and F for "false."

6 Antibiotics will not help cure a cold.   (T)   F

7 You can catch a cold by being out in the cold.   T   (F)

8 Chicken soup can help a person with a cold to feel better. (T)   F

9 Vitamin C does not have an effect on a cold.   T   (F)

Take Action!

WRITING TOPICS

Write about one of the following topics. For information about paragraph and essay structure, see the Writing Workshops (pages 127-137).

1 **Health Habits**

Write about your health habits. Also describe the health habits of a friend or family member. Discuss one or more of the following topics:

exercise   eating   relaxation

On the Companion Website, you can find evaluation grids and additional speaking and writing topics.

2 Optimist or Pessimist

Are you an optimist or a pessimist? Write a paragraph giving examples to show what type of thinking you engage in. In a second paragraph, describe somebody that you know. Explain whether that person is an optimist or a pessimist.

3 Music

In "How Singing Improves Your Health," you learned that singing is good for you. Write two paragraphs about music. First, explain whether you sing alone or in public. Explain why or why not. Then describe your favourite singer or song. Why do you like that singer or song so much?

SPEAKING TOPICS

Prepare a presentation about one of the following topics.

To listen to a discussion about technology addictions, visit the Companion Website.

1 Addictions

Listen to "Addicted to Technology" on the Companion Website. Then present an addiction that you have. It can be an addiction to Facebook, to a certain type of food, to a television program, to a certain brand, to a sport or activity, and so on. Describe what you do. Also mention when, where, and why do you do it.

2 Radio Commercial

Make a radio commercial aimed at college and university students. Convince students to take care of their health. For example, warn students about the dangers of certain drugs or convince students to exercise. Use your imagination.

3 Health TV

Work with a partner and create a health television show. You can videotape your program, use PowerPoint slides, or create posters. Each of you is responsible for discussing a particular issue. Prepare your section of the program. Do <u>one</u> of the following:

- Discuss **sports** at your college. Describe the college gymnasium and sports equipment. If you participate in college sports, describe what you do.
- Discuss the **exercise habits** of students. Ask at least five students a few questions about exercise, and describe their attitudes. Do they work out on a regular basis? Why or why not?
- Review the **food services** in your college. What are some good and bad points about the college cafeteria or café?
- Discuss **smoking habits** of students. Ask at least five students a few questions about smoking, and describe their attitudes. Do they smoke? Why or why not? Are anti-smoking campaigns working?
- Discuss **drinking and driving**. Do you know people who drink and drive? How can students be persuaded to drive safely? Survey five students.
- Discuss a health-related topic of your choice.

VOCABULARY REVIEW

Review the key terms from this chapter. Highlight the words you do not understand and learn what they mean.

- ☐ cast
- ☐ cough
- ☐ fast (v.)
- ☐ medicine
- ☐ memory
- ☐ rash
- ☐ remember
- ☐ scratch
- ☐ sneeze
- ☐ souvenir
- ☐ stutter

Visit the Companion Website to review "body parts" vocabulary. There are also practice exercises with vocabulary from this chapter.

SPEAKING PRESENTATION TIPS

- PRACTISE YOUR PRESENTATION and time yourself. You should speak for about two minutes (or for a length determined by your teacher).
- USE CUE CARDS. DO NOT READ! Put about fifteen words on your cue cards.
- BRING VISUAL SUPPORT, such as a picture, photograph, object, video, or PowerPoint slides.
- CLASSMATES WILL ASK YOU QUESTIONS about your presentation. You must also ask classmates about their presentations. Review how to form questions before your presentation day.

Revising and Editing

The Revising and Editing sections at the end of each chapter help your students prepare for writing tests, including Benchmark and TESOL tests. You can ask students to do the activities with a partner and share ideas.

REVISE FOR A MAIN IDEA

The following paragraph contains supporting details, but it has no main idea. A main idea is expressed in a topic sentence. Read the paragraph and then add a good topic sentence. (For more information about topic sentences, see Writing Workshop 1, page 127).

Topic sentence: ___Exercise has many benefits for the brain.___

First, exercise slows brain deterioration in patients who have Alzheimer's disease. According to the Canadian Broadcasting Corporation (CBC), "exercise actually slows down age-related brain cell death." Furthermore, exercise promotes brain cell growth. Finally, exercise helps the brain learn. In a Saskatoon school for at-risk students, gym equipment was put in a classroom. Before doing math, students had to work out on a treadmill for half an hour. The teacher discovered that the students had better results after they exercised. Thus, the link between exercise and the brain is becoming clear.

EDIT PRESENT TENSE VERBS

Practise editing a student paragraph. Underline and correct five errors with simple present tense verbs, not including the example.

eat

In my family, we all <u>eats</u> different food. My brother Ben <u>love</u> fresh
loves

doesn't
vegetables. He <u>don't</u> eat junk food, but sometimes he <u>have</u> sugar. Every day,
has

cooks
he <u>cook</u> his own meals. On the other hand, my sister and I love fast food.

don't
We love burgers and fries. So we usually <u>doesn't</u> eat dinner with my brother.

Don't or Doesn't

Be careful when writing negative verb forms in the simple present tense. Remember that the apostrophe replaces the o in *not*.

I, you, we, or *they*	+ *don't*	+ base form of verb
He, she, it	+ *doesn't*	+ base form of verb

We **don't** like fish.   She **doesn't** like fish.

To learn more about the simple present, see Unit 2 in *Avenues 1: English Grammar*.

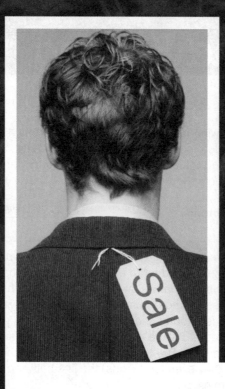

"*Our personal consumer choices have ecological, social, and spiritual consequences.*"

– DAVID SUZUKI

CHAPTER 3

Consumer Culture

What type of consumer are you? In this chapter, you will discuss and write about our consumer culture.

The Start Up provides students with practice in the present progressive tense and with the use of *there is / there are*.

Find the Differences

Join a group of four to six students. Write the names of your team members.

Team members:

_____   _____   _____

_____   _____   _____

Look at the following two photos.

A.

B.

What is different in photo B? On a separate sheet of paper, write complete sentences about six differences. Use the following vocabulary words.

| blond | brunette | shirt | heel | sleeve |

Also use the following verbs.

| try on | put on | take off | hold |

> EXAMPLE: *In Photo B, the dark-haired girl is wearing a yellow jacket.*

Grammar TIP

Present Progressive

When an action is happening right now, use the present progressive tense. It is formed with the appropriate form of *be* (*am*, *are*, *is*) and the *–ing* form of the verb. Add *not* to form negative sentences.

> They **are looking** at shoes.   The blond woman **is <u>not</u> standing**.

To learn more about the present progressive tense, see Unit 3 in *Avenues 1: English Grammar*.

 READING **STRATEGY**

Students can visit the Companion Website to practise reading strategies. Exercises on context clues, main idea, etc., are structured to help students do better in their reading tests, including Benchmark and TESOL tests.

Recognizing Context Clues

When you see an unfamiliar word, do not immediately look it up in the dictionary. You can understand the meaning of many words by looking at them in context. Consider the following points.

1. **Look at the parts of the word.** You might recognize a word part and then be able to guess the meaning (**hair**dresser).

2. **Determine the part of speech.** Sometimes it helps to know a word's function. Is it a noun, verb, adjective, and so on?

→

3. **Look at surrounding words and sentences.** Other words in the sentence can help you. Look for a synonym (a word that means the same thing) or antonym (a word that means the opposite). Also look at surrounding sentences. These may give you clues to the word's meaning.

PRACTICE

1   Determine the meaning of each word in bold.

a. Some consumers buy **trendy** clothing styles. Two months later, the trend is over and the fashion item is relegated to the bottom of the closet.

Part of speech: ___Adjective___

Clue: ___"Two months later, the trend is over."___

Meaning: ___Popular, fashionable___

b. Mr. and Mrs. Perez are extremely excited because their business **is booming**! They have more customers every day.

Part of speech: ___Verb___

Clue: ___"They have more customers every day."___

Meaning: ___Is growing___

2   Read the paragraph. Use context clues to help you find the definition of the words in bold. Circle the letter of the best definition.

Price **bundling** means selling two or more goods or services as a single package for one price. Companies **lure** consumers into buying more than they planned. A music **buff** can buy **tickets** to an **entire** concert series for a single price. A PC typically comes bundled with a monitor, a keyboard, and software.

Source: Solomon, M. R., *Marketing: Real People, Real Choices*. Upper Saddle River: Pearson, 2008. 356. Print.

1. bundling: a. opening   b. holding   c. grouping together
2. lure: a. tempt   b. write   c. send
3. buff: a. hater   b. enthusiast   c. instrument
4. tickets: a. music   b. money   c. admission coupons
5. entire: a. great   b. complete   c. cost

READING 3.1

Read about the various tricks marketers play on us. On the line opposite each highlighted word, write a short definition. Use context clues to guess the meaning of each word.

Marketing Tricks

Write definitions.

Answers will vary.

EXAMPLE:

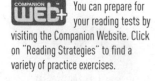
shoppers

1 You probably think that you are immune to advertising. But look at yourself. What brand of shoes are you wearing today? What type of car do you drive? What computer do you use? Chances are good that you have some brand loyalty.

2 Most consumers are attracted to certain brands without realizing why. Marketers, however, understand very well what motivates people, and they are experts at manipulating us and convincing us to spend more. Here are just some of the ways they do it.

3 **Gift Cards:** Gift cards seem like such a great idea. Instead of shopping for a gift, we present our mother with a plastic card from Sears or Future Shop, and she then picks out a gift at that store. The problem is, a lot of us shove the cards in our pocket or purse

push

and then forget about them. Consumer Reports National Research Center found that 27 percent of those who receive gift cards never use them. Businesses know that people forget, and that is why everyone from Second Cup to Victoria's Secret offers the little cards. They present a tremendous amount of easy profit for the companies that distribute them. According to Joseph T. Hallinan, in *Why We Make Mistakes*, consumers "lose about $8 billion **annually** by not redeeming gift cards."

_____yearly_____

4 **Multiple unit pricing:** An extremely effective way to get consumers to spend more is to price items in multiple units. Thus, cans of sauce are advertised as "Four for $5" rather than "One for $1.25." According to Hallinan, the number "4" acts as an anchor. "Shoppers see the number 4 and, without really thinking about it, pick up four cans."

5 **Quantity limits** are also effective at boosting sales. On a toilet paper sales rack, the "Sale: Maximum 5 per customer" works very well to increase sales. Customers think the store might run out of stock, so many people buy the maximum.

6 **Odours:** Companies use scents in marketing. Smells attract us on a primal level. Bakeries rely on the smell of baking bread to **entice** shoppers into the store. These days, many other store owners purposely inject odours into their ventilation systems, hoping the odours will encourage customers to **linger**. Bloomingdales, Lexus, and Omni Hotels are just some of the companies that pump the air with odours such as green tea and lemongrass.

_____attract_____

_____stay_____

7 **Appeals to emotion**: Most ads are not trying to reason with us; they are **targeting** our emotions. Advertisers realize that the pathway to the emotional brain is quicker than the route to the logical brain, and they use that knowledge. They hope to imprint brands on people's identities. For example, Clinton Kilts of Emory University conducted experiments on volunteers. When people saw certain brands, such as Apple or Nike, blood **rushed** to the part of the brain associated with self-identification. The product is part of their personalities.

_____aiming at_____

_____moved quickly_____

8 Brand loyalty can be stronger than product preference. L. Frank, the author of Mindfield: *How Brain Science Is Changing Our World*, says that in taste tests, most people prefer Pepsi, yet they still **purchase** Coke. Why? Coca Cola spends billions of dollars creating emotional associations with the product, and the advertising works. People like Pepsi, but Coke is associated with warm feelings of childhood.

_____buy_____

9 As a consumer, what can you do about marketing manipulation? Be conscious of your environment. If you walk into a Tim Horton's, look at the "Two chicken wrap" meal and just buy one. Ask yourself if you own your Mac laptop or if the Mac laptop owns you. **Switch** brands and try something new. Basically, pay closer attention to your purchasing decisions.

_____change_____

(621 words)

Sources: Consumer Reports National Research Center
Frank, Lone. *Mindfield: How Brain Science is Changing Our World*. Oxford: Oneworld, 2009. Print.
Hallinan, Joseph T. *Why We Make Mistakes*. New York: Broadway, 2009. Print.
Solomon, Michael R., Greg Marshall, and Elnora Stuart. *Marketing: Real People, Real Choices*. Upper Saddle River: Pearson, 2008. Print.

VOCABULARY AND COMPREHENSION

1 What is a marketing trick? Make a guess after reading the essay. (Circle the letter of the correct answer.)

a. A way that advertisers manipulate people

b. A specific advertisement

c. A company

2 Who are marketers? _____They are people who advertise products._____

3 What are two other words that mean "odours" in paragraph 6?

_____Scents_____   _____Smells_____

4 What is the main idea of the essay?

Advertisers use many skilful ways to convince people to buy products.

5 What is the main idea of paragraph 8?

a. People prefer Pepsi, but they buy Coke.

b. People have different reasons for buying products.

(c.) Sometimes people are so devoted to a brand that they will buy it even if they like a competing product better.

6 What are the supporting ideas? List them in order from 1 to 5. Put an X next to two ideas that are not in the essay.

_4_ Some business owners introduce odours into the air to influence shoppers.

_X_ Companies reduce prices on items to tempt shoppers.

_3_ Stores advertise that there are quantity limits on items, so many people then buy the maximum quantity.

_X_ Hire sports stars and singers to promote products.

_1_ Customers buy gift cards, but then they forget to actually use them.

_2_ Price items in multiple units. For instance, they offer three items for $5.

_5_ Advertisers want people to feel an emotional attachment to brands.

GRAMMAR LINK

7 Write the three questions that appear in paragraph 1.

What brand of shoes are you wearing today?

What type of car do you drive?

What computer do you use?

8 Why does only one of the questions contain an *–ing* verb?

The question about shoes refers to something that is happening today, so it uses the present

progressive tense. The questions about your car and computer refer to general facts.

🖥 WATCHING

Consumer Power

In the spring of 2008, Dave Carroll flew to Nebraska with his band. His guitar did not survive the journey. Watch the video *My Broken Guitar* about a revenge song that Dave wrote. The song went viral on YouTube, with over 3 million views in ten days.

COMPREHENSION

1 What is the name of Carroll's band?

a. Sam's Dream   b. Carroll's Boys   (c.) Sons of Maxwell

2 What is the name of Dave Carroll's song? "United Breaks Guitars"

3 Describe what happened to Carroll. Use the past tense.

He took a plane to the United States. Baggage handlers broke his guitar. United staff refused

to do anything. Carroll spent nine months trying to get the airline to do something. Then he made

a video about his experience.

4 How many songs does Carroll intend to write about the broken guitar?

a. one　　　b. two　　　ⓒ three

5 What can we learn from Dave Carroll's experience?

Answers will vary. Companies that give bad customer service should be careful, because consumers

can fight back online. Musicians can get attention by posting videos on YouTube. Music can help

to change things (his video made United pay attention to his problem).

_____

_____

DISCUSSION

1 What is a viral video? Think of some examples.

2 Why did so many people watch *My Broken Guitar* on YouTube? Think of some reasons the video became popular.

3 How is YouTube helping consumers?

 **READING 3.2**

"The Compulsive Shopper" provides students with practice identifying correct determiners, plural forms, and prepositions.

Some people take shopping to an extreme. Read about a compulsive shopper.

GRAMMAR LINK

As you read, you will see some choices in parentheses. Underline or highlight the appropriate word. Note that *X* means "nothing." On the Companion Website, you can listen to this essay and check your answers.

The Compulsive Shopper

BY R. A. PARERA

1 While walking toward a clothing store, I think, "I do not need anything." I am aware that I have enough skirts, shoes, and purses, and I know that I should not waste my money. However, as I approach the entrance, my logic suddenly changes. "I will not buy anything ... unless it is too fabulous to leave behind." Finally, I enter the store, and all logic flies out the mannequin-adorned window. Inside the store, I feel happy and optimistic, like there isn't a care in the world besides finding the perfect top.

2 Pretty much 70 percent of what I own I don't technically need. I can't even count the number of tops, pants, skirts, sweaters, or necklaces that I own. I have enough clothing to wear a completely different outfit every single (<u>day</u> / days) for two months.

3 Occasionally, I'll regret buying something. But I keep the tag on a piece of clothing until I wear it, so if I feel any regret, I'll return it. One recent item that I regretted buying was a full-body jumpsuit. It fit well but it puffed out at the hips and made me look like a fat genie. At the store, in my shopaholic haze, I thought, "I can pull this off. I can make this **wacky** outfit work." Well, once I was home and clear-minded, I realized just how very wrong I was. I returned it (a / <u>the</u>) next day, which might seem like a smart thing to do, except that instead of getting my money back, I exchanged it for two tops.

wacky: crazy

4 Although I have a shopping addiction, I am not wealthy. I graduated from college a year ago, and I work as a graphic designer. I earn just a bit over the minimum wage, and most of my salary goes toward my basic necessities. I no longer live at home, so I have to pay (<u>for</u> / X) food, rent, electricity, a bus pass, and so on. I am quite responsible. (This / <u>These</u>) days, I live on a budget and never go into debt. I do not squander large amounts of money on my shopping habit.

5 So, how do I manage to buy so (much / **many**) things? I find ways to fill my desperate craving but still keep money in the bank. I'm a bargain hunter, and there are many stores that sell very nice clothing for dirt cheap. Most of the stores I go into are very affordable. I love thrift stores and church basement sales, and I will buy second-hand clothing. At one church basement sale, I snagged a waist-length black leather jacket with silver buttons. It only cost $5, and it was the best bargain I ever found.

6 One of the (store / **stores**) that I visit has expensive clothes, but I walk straight to the sales section. I ignore everything else that I pass. I'm like a horse with blinders on. Once I'm among these inexpensive rows of clothing, and something catches my eye, I immediately look at the price and then apply the formula. If it costs as much as a meal, let's say $10 to $15, then I only need to wear it once to get my money's worth. If I'm willing to spend that money (in / **on**) food that will only satisfy me for a couple of hours, why wouldn't I spend the same on a shirt? The more I think I would wear (a / **an**) item, the more I am willing to spend. And of course there is the "beautiful" exception. If something is absolutely to die for, I will spend up to $50 depending on how obsessed I am about the object.

7 I know that I shop too much, but I like the way I live. If it makes me appear to be a shallow consumer, I'm okay with that. I know in my heart that I am not superficial.

(654 words)

VOCABULARY AND COMPREHENSION

Use context clues to determine the meanings of the following words. Do *not* use a dictionary!

1 In paragraph 1, what is the meaning of *mannequin*?

    a. A man or woman who poses for magazine photos

    (b.) A plastic representation of a human body used to display clothing

    c. A small plastic toy

2 In paragraph 2, what is the meaning of *pretty much*?

    (a.) close to   b. after   c. a lot

3 In paragraph 5, what is the meaning of *dirt cheap*? _____ Very inexpensive _____

4 In paragraph 6, what is the meaning of the expression *to die for*?

    a. really bad   b. the end   (c.) remarkable; extremely beautiful

5 In paragraph 7, Parera uses the expression *something catches my eye*. What does *catches my eye* mean? _____ Attracts my attention _____

6 Look at paragraph 7. Find a synonym or word that means the same thing as *shallow*. _____ Superficial _____

7 Why does Parera shop? What is the main reason?

    It makes her feel happy and optimistic.

8 How does she afford to buy so many clothes?

    She shops in sales sections. She finds bargains.

9 In paragraph 6, what is Parera's *formula*?

    a. It is very important to eat well, so she will spend money on meals.

    (b.) If a clothing item is the same price as a meal, she will buy it and be satisfied even if she just wears it once.

    c. The best shirts cost more than a meal, but they are really worth it.

DISCUSSION

Does the author have a shopping addiction? At what point does a shopping habit become an addiction?

Shopping Vocabulary

For sale means "available to buyers."

*My house is **for sale**.*

On sale means "available at a reduced price."

*Those pants are **on sale**. They're a bargain.*

Sell (past form: **sold**) means "to offer something in exchange for money."

*Sara **sells** jewellery on a street corner. She **sold** a lot of bracelets last night.*

PRACTICE

Fill in the blanks with the correct words from the following list. Use each choice once only.

on sale   for sale   sell   sold

1 The Bechards are moving. There is a ____for sale____ sign in front of their house.

2 If someone wants to ____sell____ a second-hand item of clothing, Marcia might buy it. Last year, a man ____sold____ a leather coat to Marcia for just $5. When Marcia shops, she searches for items that are ____on sale____ because she hates to pay the full amount.

SPEAKING

Spending Habits

Work with a partner and follow these steps:

· Ask your partner the following questions. Add one of the following auxiliaries to each question. (Remember that *be* is both a verb and an auxiliary.)

     is   are   do   does

· Write your partner's answers in the blanks.

EXAMPLES: *Where ____do____ you work?*

Answer: ____At a service station____

Partner's name: _____

1 ____Are____ you a big spender?   ☐ Yes   ☐ No

2 What ____is____ your biggest expense each month?

Answer: _____

3 ____Do____ you have a job?   ☐ Yes   ☐ No

If you answered yes, describe the job: _____

_____

4 _____Do_____ you pay rent each month? ☐ Yes ☐ No

Answer (explain why or why not): _____

_____

_____

5 _____Do_____ you have any debts? ☐ Yes ☐ No

Answer (explain why or why not): _____

_____

_____

6 What _____is_____ your most valuable possession?

Answer: _____

7 Which brands _____are_____ you loyal to?

Answer (list some brands and explain why you are loyal to them): _____

_____

_____

_____

8 What kind of life _____do_____ you want?

a) A simple life (Possessions are not important to me.)

b) A comfortable life (I want a nice house, a car, and some gadgets.)

c) A life of luxury (I want to be rich.)

WRITING

Write a paragraph about your partner's spending habits and lifestyle choices. Then write a second paragraph about yourself. **Note:** You pay **for** something. You spend money **on** something. (*Every month, I pay **for** food, and I spend money **on** rent.*)

Vocabulary BOOST

Win or *Earn*

Win (past form: **won**) means "to receive money or a prize in a contest."
*He **won** money in the lottery!*

Earn means "to make money by working."
*She **earns** the minimum wage.*

PRACTICE

Write the correct form of the verbs *win* or *earn* in the blanks.

1 Rick and Simon work in the menswear department of a large store. They _____earn_____ $12 an hour. Next year, they hope to _____earn_____ at least $15 an hour.

2 I often buy lottery tickets. I want to _____win_____ a million dollars. But I don't think that I will _____win_____, because I never _____win_____ anything. Maybe if I want money, I need to _____earn_____ it with a job.

◀))) **LISTENING PRACTICE**

The listening segments are included in the Companion Website. You can assign the listening activities in class or as homework. Please note that the audio text "Swap Culture" has different questions online.

1. Identify Large Numbers

You will hear a speaker read out some numbers. Before you listen, review how a large number is broken down.

Look at the number: **2,357,419,680**

The number breaks down as follows:

2	Two billion
357	Three hundred and fifty-seven million
419	Four hundred and nineteen thousand
680	Six hundred and eighty

The speaker will say sentences that include a number. Circle the number that is pronounced in each sentence. (Notice that the dollar symbol appears before the number.) Each sentence will be repeated.

EXAMPLE: ($40,000)/ $4000

1 ($15.95)/ $50.95

2 (1982)/ 1892

3 6418 /(6480)

4 $115.50 /($150.15)

5 1,000,000 /(1,000,000,000)

6 (40)/ 14

7 2020 /(2002)

8 ($170,000)/ $117,000

9 (13)/ 30

10 $613,000 /($630,000)

2. Pronounce Sentences

Repeat each sentence after the speaker. Then write the missing verb in the blank.

1 Consumer culture _____causes_____ problems for the environment.

2 Ben _____spends_____ a lot of money on his hobby.

3 He is a drummer, and drums _____are_____ expensive.

4 Right now, Ben _____is buying_____ drumsticks.

5 He _____isn't paying_____ with his credit card.

6 He rarely _____uses_____ his credit card.

7 Chantal _____works_____ as a cashier.

8 Right now, she _____is putting_____ the money into the cash register.

9 At this moment, Chantal _____is giving_____ Ben his change.

10 The music store _____closes_____ at 9 p.m.

◀))) **LISTENING**

Alternate questions appear in the Student Section of the Companion Website.

Swap Culture

Swap culture, or collaborative consumption, is a movement based on the principle of sharing and reusing. Listen to the interview with Anna Diaz.

Begin by listening to the first part of the interview and completing the vocabulary exercise. Then listen to the rest of the interview and answer the comprehension questions.

VOCABULARY

1 Fill in the blanks with the words that you hear in the first part of the interview.

Host: I _____am sitting_____ in the studio with Anna Diaz. She _____organizes_____ many different "collaborative consumption" initiatives. Annie, define swap culture.

Diaz: With swap culture, people _____trade_____ items. For example, right now I _____am wearing_____ a blouse that I exchanged in a clothing swap. The purse that I _____am carrying_____ came from a "free stuff" website. For travellers, _____there are_____ couch-surfing websites and home-exchange sites. Many cities, including Montreal, _____have_____ bike-sharing programs and car-sharing programs. In fact, today I _____am using_____ a shared car. Basically, swap culture is a way of life. Instead of buying more, people share what they have with others.

COMPREHENSION

Answer the following questions.

2 What does *swap* mean?

ⓐ exchange   b. sell   c. buy

3 In a junk swap, you can get rid of items. What does *get rid of* mean?

a. keep   b. sell   ⓒ discard or dispose of

4 What types of swaps does Diaz organize? Check off three answers.

☑ Clothing swaps   ☑ Furniture swaps

☐ Bike-sharing   ☐ House-sharing

☑ Junk swaps

5 How are house-sharing sites *self-policing*?

If someone is disrespectful, he or she gets removed from the site.

If someone steals or leaves a mess in someone else's home, he or she cannot use the site again.

6 Does Diaz own a home?   ☐ Yes   ☑ No

7 If you leave a house in a mess, will a home-swapping site ban you?   ☑ Yes   ☐ No

8 Why should people join swap culture? What are three good reasons?

It helps others.

It helps the environment because items get reused.

People save a lot of money.

DISCUSSION

1 Do you buy and sell items online? If so, which sites do you use? What did you buy or sell online in the past? Did you have any problems?

2 Would you be comfortable couch surfing or apartment swapping? What are some potential problems?

Why do people buy diamond wedding rings? You might be surprised to learn the real reasons behind that purchasing decision.

Diamond Marketing

BY ROBIN EDGERTON

1 In the late 1800s, the Oppenheimer family established a diamond monopoly with its company, De Beers. Around that time, Victorian culture was busy assigning abstract concepts to material objects. For instance, Kate Greenaway's wildly popular *The Language of Flowers* (1885) ascribed a meaning to each species and variety of flower. A yellow rose meant platonic love, for instance. Such symbols applied to stones as well, and they sometimes increased a stone's value. The idea that diamonds represented "perfect love" evolved during the Victorian era but was reinforced with a vengeance by the market manipulation of De Beers.

2 In the 1930s, De Beers set out to establish social status for large diamonds. The company gave a number of Hollywood starlets hefty stones. Then they arranged for glamorous photo shoots showing the star with her diamond. Hollywood movie scripts were altered to include scenes of jewellery shopping.

3 The tradition began to be manipulated more closely in one particular aspect—the act of giving. Those starlets told tales of being surprised by their large stones. Movie scenes featured a hero giving his gal a big rock and watching her eyes grow wide with joy. The diamond became a script for life, not just film. Through advertising, it became an inseparable part of courtship and marriage.

4 In 1947, De Beers' ad agency came up with the massively successful slogan, "A diamond is forever," which implied that diamonds don't crack, break, or lose value. (They do.) Diamonds became the symbol of an enduring marriage. (Before 1947, rings symbolized marriage, but the rings could be simple, without a stone.) The "Diamond is forever" slogan became so entrenched that the only proper way to "dispose" of a diamond was to hand it down to a female descendant.

5 Other techniques De Beers used are familiar today. They sent representatives to high school home economics classes to teach girls about the value of diamonds and to feed them romantic dreams. The diamond went from being a status symbol to an emotional one. A m an's love for his wife could be measured in carats.

6 Ten-year anniversary rings were created and heavily advertised in the 1960s after De Beers was forced to purchase large stocks of Russian diamonds. Most of these diamonds were small white gems of less than one-quarter carat. Previously, De Beers pushed engagement rings with larger (and mostly South African) stones. They had to adjust their campaigns. Hence, the eternity ring—equally expensive but with smaller stones—was marketed specifically for anniversaries.

7 In 1967, De Beers contacted advertising agency J. Walter Thompson to popularize the diamond engagement ring in Brazil, Germany, and Japan. While De Beers found limited success in the former two countries, Japan far exceeded expectations. By 1978, half of all Japanese brides received a diamond engagement ring. By 1981, the number grew to 60 percent; the "tradition" had taken hold. Just how did the J. Walter Thompson agency accomplish this? In a basic but general ad campaign similar to that in the U.S.—the diamond ring was pitched not as a product but as a symbol.

(517 words)

Source: Edgerton, Robin. "Engagement, Inc.: The Marketing of Diamonds." *Stay Free!* Stay Free Magazine. Issue 16. Web.

Additional questions for "Diamond Marketing" appear in the Student Section of the Companion Website.

VOCABULARY AND COMPREHENSION

1 Choose the letters of the best definitions. The paragraph numbers are in parentheses.

Terms		Definitions
1. altered (2)	c	a. long-lasting
2. starlet (2)	e	b. advertising phrase
3. gal (3)	d	c. changed
4. enduring (4)	a	d. girlfriend
5. slogan (4)	b	e. young Hollywood actress

2 Why do most men give their brides a diamond ring today?

A diamond company successfully convinced people that it is necessary.

3 What marketing strategies did De Beers use to get people to buy diamonds? List three steps they took.

First, they gave rings to Hollywood stars and made diamonds equal higher social status.

Then they featured diamond-giving in Hollywood movie scenes. Finally, they used the

"A diamond is forever" campaign to show that diamonds symbolize an enduring marriage.

4 Did diamonds always symbolize romantic love?   ☐ Yes   ☑ No

5 Look at paragraph 1. Underline a sentence that expresses the main idea of the essay.

GRAMMAR LINK

6 Highlight three irregular past tense verbs in paragraph 3. Then write the past and present form of the three verbs here.

1. Past: _____began_____   Present: _____begin_____

2. Past: _____told_____   Present: _____tell_____

3. Past: _____became_____   Present: _____become_____

DISCUSSION

1 De Beers had the most successful marketing strategy of all time. Do you agree? Explain your answer.

2 Think about other items that people feel pressured to buy. What items are status symbols?

3 Will you buy a diamond wedding ring or will you expect to receive one? Explain your answer.

🖵 WATCHING

Pook Toques

On *Dragons' Den*, aspiring entrepreneurs pitch their business concepts and products to a panel of Canadian business moguls. Watch the episode and answer the questions.

Kevin   Jim   Arlene   Robert   Brett

You can assign *Pook Toques* in class or as homework. On the Companion Website, students can watch the video and answer additional questions of medium difficulty. You can check their scores with the grade tracker.

COMPREHENSION

1 Where are Tony Pook and Kevin McCotter from?

(a.) St. Mary's, Ontario   b. St. John's, Newfoundland   c. Kimberley, BC

2 What main product are they selling? _____Sock hats_____

3 What are some of the Pook Toque styles? Put a check mark (✓) beside four names they use.

☑ Executive   ☑ Shrek

☑ Rastafarian   ☐ Mickey Mouse

☐ Justin Bieber   ☑ Robin Hood

4 How much does a Pook Toque cost?

a. About $10   (b.) About $20   c. About $30

5 The Pook Toque creators made a special toque for each dragon. Write the letter of the toque given to each dragon.

1. Jim   ___b___   a. Donald Trump comb-over

2. Brett   ___c___   b. Double-dip donut

3. Kevin   ___a___   c. Cowboy mullet

6 Where do the Pook Toque men sell their hats? _____Craft shows and The Bay_____

7 What were their revenues last year?

a. $40,000   (b.) $400,000   c. $4 million

8 According to Pook Toque owners, what is the value of their company?

_____$2.5 million_____

9 Kevin and Brett comment on the evaluation. What is their opinion?

a. The evaluation is good and realistic.

(b.) The evaluation is crazy and not realistic.

10 Robert makes an offer. He offers $250,000 for how much of the business?

_____50 percent_____

VOCABULARY

After you watch the video, guess what the highlighted vocabulary terms mean by considering the context. Use logic when you make your choices.

11 The sock hat is our **flagship** product, but we have other products too.

a. cheap   (b.) main; prominent   c. only

12 The hat is "the Donald Trump **comb-over**."

a. A type of clothing

(b.) A hairstyle: hair is combed to cover up a bald spot

c. A type of building

13 Your evaluation is **nuts**.

(a.) crazy; not realistic   b. good; realistic   c. unusual

14 I think you have a very quick **fad**. I think you can make a lot of money over a short period of time.

a. product   b. money   (c.) something that is temporarily in style

15 Let's see if they have got a **counter**-offer up their sleeves.

(a.) alternative   b. happy   c. impossible

DISCUSSION

1. Did the Pook Toque inventors take the deal? Why or why not?
2. In your opinion, did Robert offer a good deal or a bad deal? Explain your answer.
3. Is the Pook Toque a good or a bad product? Give your opinion.

You might ask students to do a speaking presentation about a trend. In the Take Action! section on page 50, Topic 3 can be a formal speaking test.

... SPEAKING

Interview about Trends

Discuss the following questions with a partner. Add the correct auxiliary to each question. Insert one of the following auxiliaries.

| do | does | is | are | did | was | were |

Then write your partner's answers on the lines.

Partner's name: _____

Discussing the Past

1. During your childhood, what _____were_____ the most popular fashions? You can describe hair, clothing, and shoe styles for men and women.

   Men's fashions: _____
   _____
   _____

   Women's fashions: _____
   _____
   _____

2. During your childhood, what technological products _____were_____ popular? Describe them.

   _____
   _____

3. When you were a child, what _____did_____ typical cars look like? Consider the size, colours, and marks of cars.

   _____
   _____

Discussing the Present

4. What styles _____are_____ popular today? Think about hair, clothing, and shoe styles for men and women.

   Men's fashions: _____
   _____
   _____

   Women's fashions: _____
   _____
   _____

5 What technological products _____do_____ people use today? List at least five items.

_____

_____

6 What _____do_____ cars look like today? How _____are_____ they different from past cars? Describe them.

_____

_____

Take Action!

On the Companion Website, you can find evaluation grids and additional speaking and writing topics.

WRITING TOPICS

Write about one of the following topics. For information about paragraph and essay structure, see the Writing Workshops on pages 127-140.

1 Personal Style

Describe your style and the style of someone you know. Write two paragraphs.

- In your first paragraph, describe yourself. What are you wearing right now? What clothes or fashions do you like or dislike? Where do you shop? Give examples.

- In your second paragraph, describe a friend or family member. What is he or she wearing today? What is that person's style? What type of shopper is that person?

2 Brands and Status Symbols

Maybe you heard about the American dream? Well, what is the Canadian dream? Write about ideal lifestyles and about status symbols.

- First, describe the Canadian dream. What do all Canadians hope to achieve? Also describe the lifestyle that you want. How important is money to you?

- Then discuss status symbols and popular brands. For instance, think about shoe, computer, car, or clothing brands. Why are some brands so popular? What are current status symbols? Which brands do you buy?

- Finally, describe a time in the past when you bought something because it was popular. For example, did you buy a particular brand of running shoes or a certain style of cellphone? Was it a good or bad decision to buy that item? Explain why.

3 Spending Habits

Write an essay about your spending habits.

- First, describe your past spending habits. Were you a saver or a spender? Did your parents give you an allowance? Did you do chores to earn money? What types of things did you buy?

- Then describe your spending habits today. How do you earn money? Do your parents support you? Do you have a student loan, or do you work part-time? What do you spend your money on?

SPEAKING TOPICS

Prepare a presentation about one of the following topics.

You can make this a writing activity. Ask students to write their sentences under a photograph.

1 Every Picture Tells a Story

Look in your photo album or online for a picture that has the following elements. You can look on *flickr.com* or any photo website.

· There must be at least three people in the picture.

· The people must be doing different actions.

· The people must be in an identifiable place.

Invent a story about the people in the picture. Use the simple present and the present progressive tenses in your story.

EXAMPLE: *The man's name **is** Thomas. He **works** in a bank. He **is talking** with his girlfriend, Julia. Julia **is laughing** because …*

For the *Dragons' Den* activity, you can ask students to work in pairs or groups. Groups can brainstorm product ideas and then present a product to another team.

2 Dragons' Den

(Optional: Work with a partner or a team of students.)

Think of a new fashion or product and propose it to *Dragons' Den*. As a suggestion, you can combine two pieces of clothing into one or combine two products into one, just as the "sock hat" inventors did. Be prepared to talk about the following:

a. Explain who you are marketing your product to.

b. Determine a price for your product.

c. Determine a value for your company. Then decide how much money you need to ask for.

d. Describe the best features of your item.

e. Explain what you are doing these days to promote your item. (Use your imagination.)

You must answer questions about your product. You will also ask other team members about their products. Your team will have a chance to be both the inventors and the dragons.

The "Trends" topic works well as a mid-term or final speaking test.

3 Trends

A trend is something that is very popular for a short period of time. Present trends from the past, present, and future.

a. Describe a trend from your childhood. Describe a clothing, shoe, or hair fashion, or describe a product such as a game, car, or technological item. Describe something that was very popular for a short period of time.

b. Describe a present trend. Describe clothing, shoes, or hair fashions, or a product such as a game, car, or technological item. Choose something that is very popular these days.

c. Predict a future trend. What will everyone buy next year?

VOCABULARY REVIEW

Review key terms from this chapter. Identify the words you do not understand and learn what they mean.

☐ bargain	☐ on sale
☐ consumer	☐ put on
☐ dirt cheap	☐ sell
☐ earn	☐ take off
☐ expense	☐ trick
☐ fad	☐ win

web+ To practise vocabulary from this chapter, visit the Companion Website.

SPEAKING PRESENTATION TIPS

· PRACTISE YOUR PRESENTATION and time yourself. You should speak for about two minutes (or for a length determined by your teacher).

· USE CUE CARDS. DO NOT READ! Put about fifteen words on your cue cards.

· BRING VISUAL SUPPORT, such as a picture, photograph, object, video, or PowerPoint slides.

· CLASSMATES WILL ASK YOU QUESTIONS about your presentation. You must also ask classmates about their presentations. Review how to form questions before your presentation day.

Revising and Editing

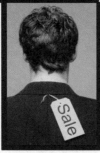

The Revising and Editing sections at the end of each chapter help your students prepare for writing tests, including Benchmark and TESOL tests. You can ask students to do the activities with a partner and share ideas.

REVISE FOR TRANSITIONS

A good paragraph should have transitional words to link ideas. The following paragraph does not flow because it has no transitions. Add the following words in the appropriate spaces. (To learn more about transitional words and phrases, see Writing Workshop 3 on page 139.)

~~first~~   finally   of course   then
for example   in fact   to conclude

I am changing my spending habits. _____*First*_____, I destroyed my credit cards. _____In fact_____, I put my Master Card and my Bay card in the shredder last week. _____Then_____ I made a budget. _____

_____Of course_____, I do not always stick to my budget, but I try to.

_____Finally_____, I am selling old items before I buy any new ones.

_____For example_____, if I want a new iPhone, I must sell other items until I have enough to buy the iPhone. _____To conclude_____, I am really making an effort to change and to consume less.

EDIT PRESENT PROGRESSIVE VERBS

Practise editing a student paragraph. Underline and correct five errors with present progressive verbs, not including the example.

            am wearing   carrying
Right now, I wearing Nike runners. Melissa is carry a purse from Urban

                   is listening   are promoting
Outfitters, and Samuel listening to an iPod. We promoting some brands.

             are
Of course, we is not trying to advertise products, but people see what

      are wearing
we wearing. We live in a brand culture, and we are part of the problem.

Grammar TIP

Use Complete Verbs

With present progressive verbs, use the correct form of the verb *be* (*am*, *are*, *is*). Also, ensure that the main verb ends in *–ing*.

   is   *waiting*
She **buying** some new shoes. Her friends are **~~wait~~** for her.

To learn more about the present progressive tense, see Unit 3 in *Avenues 1: English Grammar*.

CHAPTER 4

> "More than a third of species ...
> are threatened with extinction.
> These include 21 percent of
> all known mammals and
> 30 percent of amphibians."
>
> – UN BIODIVERSITY
> CONSERVATION GROUP

Into the Wild

Which natural environment do you prefer?
Could you survive in the wild? In this
chapter, you will reflect on the world
of nature.

Connection with Nature

Work with a partner or a group of students, and discuss the following questions. Talk without stopping about the following topics.

1 Discuss your preferences. Would you rather ...

- spend the weekend indoors or outdoors?
- live in the city or country?
- live beside a desert, beach, mountain, or forest?

2 If you are lost in the woods, and you have no matches or lighter, how do you start a fire?

3 Which trees can you identify? List some.

4 Which two types of berries are poisonous? Choose two of the photos.

You can tell the students that A (blueberries) and C (gooseberries) are edible. B (yew berries) and D (pokeweed berries) are toxic.

A  **B**  **C**  **D**

5 If you go camping in the wilderness, what are the ten most important items to bring with you? List ten essential items.

READING STRATEGY

Students can visit the Companion Website to practise reading strategies. Exercises on context clues, main idea, etc., are structured to help students do better in their reading tests, including Benchmark and TESOL tests.

wEB+ You can prepare for your reading tests by visiting the Companion Website. Click on "Reading Strategies" to find a variety of practice exercises.

Using a Dictionary

Use a dictionary only when you cannot understand a word from the context in which it appears. When you consult a dictionary, remember the following:

1. Read all of the meanings and choose the logical one. Some words have more than one definition. For example, *wind* means "blowing air," but it also means "to bend or turn." Read the word in context and you should be able to identify the correct definition.

2. Determine the part of speech. For instance, imagine that you do not know the meaning of *fine* in the sentence: "He received a fine." Your dictionary has three definitions: *fine* (adj.), *fine* (n.), and *fine* (v.). You would look at the noun definition.

PRACTICE

Use your dictionary—or go to *dictionary.reference.com*—to define the words in bold. Check multiple definitions and consider the part of speech before you write your definition.

1 The giraffes live in the **wild**. _Uninhabited region in nature_

2 Do not go near the **wild** dog. _Not tamed or domesticated_

3 The hunters decided to **pelt** the protestors with rocks. _Attack_

4 The actress will not wear an animal **pelt**. _Animal hide or fur_

 Listen to the essay "Into the Wild."

Could you survive alone in the woods? Read about one woman's reflections on these questions.

GRAMMAR LINK

In paragraphs 1 and 2, fill in the blanks with the correct past tense forms of the verbs in parentheses. You can listen to this essay on the Companion Website and check your answers.

Into the Wild

BY D. KIRBY

1 A few weeks ago, I (watch) _____ watched _____ the heartbreaking movie *Into the Wild*. It tells the true-life story of a young adventurer. In 1992, an idealistic young American, Christopher McCandless, (leave) _____ left _____ the comfort of home and family to live in the wild. He (give) _____ gave _____ away his worldly goods. He also (stop) _____ stopped _____ all contact with his family. Alone on the road, he (hold) _____ held _____ up his thumb and hitchhiked to Alaska.

2 Deep in the Alaska woods, far from civilization, McCandless (find) _____ found _____ an abandoned trailer. Unfortunately, he (be) _____ was _____ hopelessly unprepared. He (know, not) _____ did not know _____ the difference between an edible plant and a poisonous one, even when he (have) _____ had _____ a guidebook to show him the differences. Of course, poisonous plants and edible plants can look similar. When he was starving, McCandless killed a moose, but he left the meat in the sun for too long, and the meat became infested with **maggots**. Even though he was hungry, he (feel) _____ felt _____ terrible about the killing and called it "the worst mistake" of his life.

3 The movie made me reflect on my own disconnect with the wild. I'm a city girl. I don't know the names of flowers or trees. After a lifetime of living in Canada, I still don't know a spruce tree from a pine. If I landed in a forest tonight, I would not know an edible mushroom from a poisonous one. I can't build my own shelter or make a fire without matches. I don't know how to build a trap, and, like Christopher McCandless, I would be squeamish about killing an animal.

4 The only time I ever tried to "survive" in the wild was during a camping trip. Unfortunately, I didn't protect my tent from the rain. A storm soaked all of my clothing and my sleeping bag, so I packed up and left the next morning. Basically, if you put me in the woods and my shoes get **wet**, I want to go back to civilization.

5 This all got me to thinking that I should be more prepared. I decided to do some research, and I found some great survival tips from a tough Australian guy, Bear Grylls. He says that if you are lost somewhere, the first thing you need to do is find shelter, then water, and then food.

6 If you are ever lost in the desert, Grylls has good advice. He suggests that you keep your clothes on even if you are really hot. Your clothes protect you from the sun and delay the possible onset of **sunstroke**. Your sweat actually has a cooling effect on your body. Your head is the most important part of the body to keep cool, according to Grylls. You can wrap light-coloured clothing around it. On his website, Grylls advises, "Keep your shirt on your back, and take off your underpants and wear them on your head. You might look a bit **daft**, but you won't die quite as fast."

Scene from the movie *Into the Wild*

maggots: larvae (immature form) of insects

wet: soaked with water

sunstroke: overheated body temperature that can lead to convulsions and coma

daft: ridiculous

7 What should you do when you need protein but you are alone in the woods? Bear Grylls says that you should never go for big **game** because the chances are too high that the meat will go rotten before you can eat it. Instead, Grylls suggests eating rats. He claims that he survived in a Chinese jungle by eating rats' brains.

8 If you are lost in a forest, and if the trees are quite dense, climb the tallest tree and find your bearings. And this next bit of advice I liked the best. According to Grylls, "If you can't swim well but you need to cross a large body of water, you can use your pants as a flotation device. Remove your pants, tie off the legs, and fill them with air. Raise the pants over your head in the water. The pants will act like a **life jacket**."

9 *Into the Wild* made me realize how **woefully** disconnected many of us are from the natural world. The fact is, most of us won't do what McCandless did. We won't walk alone into a forest because we are unable to survive in truly natural surroundings. Most of us would rather stay indoors, with our cellphones and laptops, than venture out into the wild. Maybe that's the saddest fact of all.

(743 words)

VOCABULARY AND COMPREHENSION

1 Look at the following words in context, and then guess their meanings. The paragraph numbers are in parentheses. Write the letters of the correct definitions in the spaces provided.

Terms		**Definitions**
1. poisonous (2)	c	a. building or temporary refuge
2. squeamish (3)	e	b. perspiration
3. soaked (4)	d	c. toxic
4. shelter (5)	a	d. saturated with water
5. sweat (6)	b	e. disgusted or nauseated

2 In paragraph 8, what is the meaning of *find your bearings*?

Figure out where you are

3 Who was Christopher McCandless? He was a young American who left his home and went to live in the wild. Someone made a movie about him.

4 What is Bear Grylls's advice if you are in the following situations?

a. You are hungry and need protein. Eat small animals such as rats.

b. You are alone in a desert. Keep your clothing on and cover your head.

c. You are lost in the woods. Climb the tallest tree to find where you are.

d. You want to cross a river. Use your pants as a flotation device.

WRITE DEFINITIONS AND QUESTIONS

Using a separate sheet of paper, follow these instructions.

1 Choose five difficult words from the text and write a definition for each word.

2 Write six questions that you would like to ask Bear Gryllis, the Australian survival specialist. Write at least three questions using the past tense.

Woods and *Nature*

Wood is from a tree and is used as a building material.

(This is a non-count noun and has no plural form.)

The **woods** are an area with many trees, such as a forest.

Nature does not require *the* before it. But you can say "the natural world."

> *Bruce bought some **wood** and built a table. Then he went for a walk in the **woods**. He likes **nature**. In fact, he loves **the natural world**.*

PRACTICE

Correct four errors in the sentences.

Christopher McCandless went alone into the wood. (woods) He wanted to live in the (the̶) nature, away from people. He decided to build a small shelter out of woods. (wood)

He really loved natural world. (the)

🔊 **LISTENING PRACTICE**

1. Pronounce Past Tense Verbs

Regular past tense verbs end in *–ed*. There are three different ways to pronounce the final *–ed* ending.

Regular Past Tense Verbs

RULES	PAST TENSE ENDING SOUNDS LIKE	EXAMPLES		
When the verb ends in an *s, k, f, p, x, ch,* or *sh* sound, the final *–ed* is pronounced *t*:	**t**	asked	kissed	wished
When the verb ends in *t* or *d*, the final *–ed* is pronounced as a separate syllable.	**id**	wanted	added	folded
In all other regular verbs, the final *–ed* is pronounced *d*.	**d**	lived	aged	moved

Repeat each verb twice after the speaker. Then indicate if the verb ends with a *t*, *d*, or *id* sound.

EXAMPLE: *added*   t   d   (id)

1	asked	(t)	d	id	6 missed	(t)	d	id
2	needed	t	d	(id)	7 counted	t	d	(id)
3	discussed	(t)	d	id	8 baked	(t)	d	id
4	opened	t	(d)	id	9 tried	t	(d)	id
5	divided	t	d	(id)	10 landed	t	d	(id)

2. Pronounce Sentences and Identify Verbs

Review how to pronounce certain irregular past tense verbs.

Irregular Past Tense Verbs

RULE	SOUND	EXAMPLES
When the past tense verb ends in *–ought* or *–aught,* pronounce the final letters as *ot.*	**ot**	bought taught caught

Repeat each sentence after the speaker. Then fill in the blanks with the missing verbs.

1   We _____ walked _____ into the woods.

2   My father _____ brought _____ a lot of camping supplies.

3   We _____ decided _____ to build a fire.

4   We went to a lake and _____ caught _____ some fish.

5   During the night, we _____ thought _____ that there was a strange sound.

6   My brother _____ looked _____ outside and saw a bear.

7   He _____ asked _____ my father a question.

8   My father _____ suggested _____ that we stay completely still.

9   We were scared, so we _____ counted _____ the seconds.

10   The next day, my brother _____ wanted _____ to leave.

The listening segments are included in the Companion Website. You can assign the listening activities in class or give them as homework. Please note that "The Vegetarian and the Meat Eater" has different questions online.

◀)) **LISTENING**

The Vegetarian and the Meat Eater

Beth Lewis is a vegetarian, and Mark Kalzan is a meat eater. Listen to the interview.

PRE-LISTENING VOCABULARY

Before you listen, review the meanings of the following words.

- **cattle:**   cows
- **manure:**   animal excrement
- **greenhouse gases:** emissions that contribute to global warming
- **industrial plant:** factory
- **brain:**   organ in the head that controls mental and physical actions

COMPREHENSION

In the spaces, insert the five main arguments of each speaker.

Reasons	Beth Lewis	Mark Kalzan
Ethical / spiritual	Animals have feelings and suffer.	Meat tastes good.
Health	Vegetarians have lower fat and cholesterol levels. Vegetarians live longer.	Flour and refined sugar are bad for the health. Meat has vitamin B12.
Environment	Animal farms produce methane, which is a greenhouse gas. Forests are destroyed.	Houses take away animal habitats.
Living conditions	Industrial animals are in small cages. They are tortured.	People live in unsanitary crowded places too.
Other moral reasons	Giving up meat can help reduce world poverty. Grain that goes to cattle can go to people instead.	Meat helped the human brain to grow. It is part of human history.

 **SPEAKING**

Ethics and Animals

Unscramble the words in each question. Then ask a partner to answer the questions. Write your partner's answers on the lines.

Partner's name: _____

Grammar TIP

Question Forms

Always ensure that your questions have the proper word order.

Question word + auxiliary + subject + verb
When   did   you   leave the city?

To learn more about question forms, see *Avenues 1: English Grammar.*

1. Which foods (you, do, eat, usually) __do you usually eat_____? (Indicate your partner's choices.)

   ☐ pork   ☐ beef   ☐ lamb   ☐ chicken   ☐ fish   ☐ tofu   ☐ veggies

2. (you, are, a vegetarian) __Are you a vegetarian_____?

   Answer (explain why or why not): _____

   _____

3. (wear, do, leather, you) __Do you wear leather_____?

   Answer (explain why or why not): _____

   _____

4 (you, wear, would, a fur coat) _____ Would you wear a fur coat _____?

Answer (explain why or why not): _____

_____

5 (you, would, kill an animal) _____ Would you kill an animal _____?

Answer (explain why or why not): _____

_____

6 Why (many species, becoming extinct, are) _____ are many species becoming extinct _____

_____?

Answer (list at least three causes): _____ Hunting for sport, for medicine, and for illegal

trading / Loss of land (animal habitats) and pollution (e.g., gulf oil spill) / Food industry

(some endangered animals are delicacies)

WRITING

In a paragraph of about 120 words, describe your partner's opinions and preferences.

Grammar TIP

Using *Would*

You can use the auxiliary *would* to express a possible action. Use the base form of the verb after *would*.

*Under the right conditions, she **would kill** an animal.*

To learn more about the modal forms, see Unit 9 in *Avenues 1: English Grammar*.

📖 READING 4.2

You can assign "The Emotional Lives of Animals" in class or as homework. Different questions for these readings appear on the Companion Website.

Can animals feel? Do they have anything close to human emotions? Read two essays about the animal world.

PAIR READING ACTIVITY (OPTIONAL)

Find a partner. One of you will read Part A, "Animal Love and Friendship," and the other will read Part B, "Animal Altruism." Then answer the questions that follow your reading. Later, you will share information with your partner.

PRE-READING VOCABULARY

First, review some vocabulary used in the part of the essay that you will be reading. Write the correct word under each photo.

PART A

trunk   goose   nest   goat

goat   trunk   nest   goose

grass   fence   tusk   stick

stick   grass   fence   tusk

The Emotional Lives of Animals

PART A – ANIMAL LOVE AND FRIENDSHIP

calf: baby elephant
banks: land beside the river

rocky ledge: flat protruding piece
of stone

1 Only humans, it is said, feel noble emotions such as true love. But there are instances of wild animals showing devotion. For example, in the 1930s, in Burma, J. H. Williams observed a mother elephant saving her three-month-old calf. They were trapped in rising floodwaters, and the banks of the river were fifteen feet high. Using her trunk, the mother elephant held the baby against her body. The water kept rising, so she stood on her hind legs and placed her calf on a rocky ledge above the water. Then the mother fell back into the torrent and disappeared downstream. Half an hour later, the mother ran beside the river, calling out. When she saw her calf still on the ledge, she rumbled—a sound elephants make when they are pleased. In the morning, the river was not flooding anymore, so the elephant reclaimed her calf.

2 Some young animals show attachment to their parents. Jane Goodall describes the reaction of a male chimpanzee called Flint, who was eight years old when his mother, Flo, died. Flint sat over Flo's body for many hours and occasionally tugged at her hand. As the days passed, he grew more lethargic. Flint died a few months later. Goodall's scientific conclusion did not mention feelings, but her common sense evaluation was "Flint died of grief."

gander: male goose

3 In some species, animals mate and then separate. But geese will pair for life. Konrad Lorenz described the behaviour of Ado, a gander, when a fox killed its mate Suzanne. Ado stood silently by his mate's partly eaten body, which lay across their nest. In the following days, Ado stopped eating. His status in the flock plummeted, since he did not defend himself from the attacks of the other geese. A year later, Ado pulled himself together and met another goose.

4 Generally, animals are not friendly toward other species. However, exceptions occur when animals are held in captivity with other animals. For instance, it is common for horses to make friends with other animals such as goats. There are examples

mope: act sad and depressed

of horses that mope when separated from their goat friends.

5 These instances and more suggest that animals have strong bonds with each other.

(364 words)

Source: Adapted from Moussaieff Masson, J. and Susan McCarthy. *When Elephants Weep: The Emotional Lives of Animals.* New York: Delta. 1995. Print.

VOCABULARY AND COMPREHENSION

1 Match the words with the best definitions. The paragraph numbers are in parentheses. Read the words in context before you make your guess.

Terms		Definitions
1. trapped (1)	d	a. back
2. hind (1)	a	b. sorrow or mourning after a death or other sad loss
3. tugged (2)	e	c. fell quickly
4. grief (3)	b	d. not able to move
5. plummeted (3)	c	e. pulled

2 Ado and Suzanne are what type of animals? Give the singular and plural forms.

Singular form: _____goose_____ · Plural form: _____geese_____

3 In paragraph 3, what does *pulled himself together* mean?

a. removed his nest

b.) recovered after an emotional trauma

4 What is the main idea of this text? (The main idea is the principal message.)

a. Chimpanzees feel very attached to their mothers.

b. All animals show love.

c.) Some animals show strong feelings—what appears to be love—toward other animals.

Answers will vary.

5 Give examples of how each of the anecdotes supports the main idea.

Burmese elephant: __The mother elephant risked her life to save her baby.__

Chimp: __A young chimp showed deep sadness and depression when its mother died.__

Goose: __A gander took a very long time to get over the death of its mate.__

Horse: __Horses bond with animals of other species, such as goats, and act sad and depressed when their companion is not there.__

The Emotional Lives of Animals

PART B – ANIMAL ALTRUISM

1 Occasionally, animals display altruistic behaviour. An example involves a chimpanzee called Washoe. The chimp lived on an island in an animal park. [Chimps are afraid of water, so they are often kept on small islands.] One day, a female chimpanzee was introduced to the park. Scared, she jumped over the electric fence that surrounds the island and fell into the water. Unable to swim, she panicked. Researcher Roger Fouts decided to rescue her. But before he could act, Washoe ran to the fence, leapt over it, and landed on the narrow **bank**. Washoe held onto the grass with one hand and pulled the female chimp to safety. Fouts said, "I was headed into the water, ready to go in after her. Washoe beat me to it. So I guess Washoe and I were reacting to the same stimulus—'individual in trouble.'"

bank: land bordering a body of water

2 Sometimes animals will rescue other species. One evening in Kenya, human observers saw a black rhinoceros mother. Her six-month-old calf got mired in some deep mud. The mother rhinoceros, unsure what to do, left the calf and walked into the woods.

3 Then some elephants arrived. An elephant with large tusks approached the baby rhino. It knelt down and put its tusks under the baby rhino's belly, and began to lift it. The mother rhino, thinking her calf was in danger, charged out of the woods, so the elephant quickly moved away. Over several hours, whenever the mother rhino left, the elephant tried to rescue the baby rhino. But each time, the mother rhinoceros rushed out protectively. Eventually, the elephants moved on. The next morning, the baby rhino managed to free itself.

4 In the 1960s, researcher Geza Teleki followed a group of wild chimps. Mr. Teleki forgot to bring his lunch, so he used a stick to try to knock some fruit off a tree. Chimpanzees were eating in a nearby tree, and they watched the human. Teleki continued to jump and hit the tree branches with a stick, but no fruit fell. After ten minutes, feeling discouraged, he gave up. Suddenly, to Teleki's surprise, an adolescent male chimpanzee collected some fruit, climbed down from the tree, and gave the food to Teleki.

5 The examples suggest that animals are capable of helping others, with no benefit to themselves.

(379 words)

Source: Adapted from Moussaieff Masson, J. and Susan McCarthy. *When Elephants Weep: The Emotional Lives of Animals*. New York: Delta. 1995. Print.

VOCABULARY AND COMPREHENSION

1 Match the words with the best definitions. The paragraph numbers are in parentheses. Read the words in context before you make your guess.

Terms		**Definitions**
1. rescue (1)	b	a. ran toward something aggressively
2. leapt (present tense: *leap*) (1)	e	b. save
3. mired (2)	d	c. hit
4. charged (3)	a	d. stuck; unable to move
5. knocked (4)	c	e. jumped

2 In paragraph 1, who saved the chimp that was in the water?

a. Roger Fouts (the researcher)   (b.) Washoe (the chimp)

3 In paragraph 1, what does *beat me to it* mean?

a. hit me

(b.) got there first and acted before I could

4 What is the main idea of this text? (The main idea is the central message.)

a. Chimpanzees are very intelligent and will help other animals.

b. All animals are generous and kind to other animals.

(c.) Sometimes certain animals demonstrate altruism; they help others when there is no benefit to themselves.

5 Give examples of how each anecdote supports the main idea. Answers will vary.

Washoe: _Washoe saved another chimp from drowning._

The rhino and the elephant: _An elephant tried to save a baby rhino that was stuck in mud._

Teleki and the chimp: _A chimpanzee collected fruit for a hungry human._

PAIR READING: SHARE INFORMATION

Work with a student who has read the other text, and share information.

1 What do the following terms or expressions mean? Write a definition or translation.

a. grief ___Sorrow or mourning after a death or other sad loss___

b. rescue ___Save___

c. hind legs ___Back legs___

d. tusk ___Protruding horn___

e. beat me to it ___Get there first and act before I can___

f. pull yourself together ___Recover after an emotional trauma___

2 Tell your partner about what you read. (You can briefly summarize each anecdote.) Also listen to your partner's summary. On a separate sheet of paper, write what your partner tells you.

In the Teacher Section of the Companion Website, there is a reading test called "Is It Love or a Trick?" The essay discusses how dogs manipulate people. If you assign that reading test, you can have a discussion afterwards. Students can talk about Reading 4.2, and then consider if the reading test is contradictory. They can discuss whether dogs have feelings or are simply manipulative.

🖥 WATCHING

As a suggestion, you can assign this video as homework. Students can visit the Companion Website to watch the video and answer fifteen questions. Note that some of the same questions appear in this book. You can verify that the homework was done by looking at the grade tracker.

Christian the Lion

In 1969, John Rendall and Anthony "Ace" Bourke bought a baby lion. The lion was reintroduced to the African wild, and the lion's return was filmed for a 1971 documentary. Many years later, someone posted a clip from the documentary on YouTube, and the *Christian the Lion* video became a worldwide sensation.

COMPREHENSION

1 Two men, John Rendall and Anthony Bourke, bought a lion. What nationality are the men?

a. German
(b.) Australian
c. Canadian

2 Where did the two men find the lion? _In a department store_

3 What happened after they brought the lion home? _They cared for it, but then it grew too large. They decided to set it free in Africa._

4 Bourke and Rendall met George Adamson. What book did George and Joy Adamson write?

a. *Back to Africa*   b. *Lion Life*   ⓒ *Born Free*

5 After a year apart, the two men wanted to visit their lion in Africa. What did experts tell them?

a. It is a great idea. Your lion will remember you.

ⓑ You are putting your lives in danger. The lion will not remember you.

6 When the men went to Africa to visit the lion, what happened?

The lion recognized their voices and ran to them and jumped up on them.

7 When was *Christian the Lion* put on YouTube?

a. 2001   b. 2004   ⓒ 2007

8 What is Eric Cole's opinion of the story about Christian the lion?

ⓐ It is an exceptional occurrence. Usually, people cannot domesticate lions.

b. It is not unusual. Humans often domesticate wild lions.

📖 **READING 4.3**

In a four-part series, Thomas French chronicled life inside Lowry Park Zoo in Tampa, Florida. Read the following excerpt.

Zoo Story

BY THOMAS FRENCH

1 A chimpanzee named Herman is the zoo's most famous resident. Born in Africa and raised as a family pet for the first few years of his life, he has reigned at Lowry Park for **three decades**. He arrived in the early '70s, when Lowry Park was considered one of the most **wretched** zoos in the United States, and he watched in the late '80s as the original cages were replaced with more progressive, open exhibits.

2 Herman is approaching forty now. He moves more slowly than he used to, but he still declares his dominance with a series of repeated displays. He rocks from side to side, waves his arms, and marches back and forth like a general parading. If he sees someone touch one of the female **keepers**, he throws dirt and pounds his body against the walls of the exhibit. "We better move out of sight," the keeper will say.

3 Herman suffers from an identity crisis. He does not appear to fully understand that he is a chimp. His early years, when he was clothed and treated like a human child, have left him in profound confusion. Several female chimps are sexually available to him, but he is attracted only to human females. This is disastrous for him because it prevents him from ever **mating** or joining his own species. Surrounded by other chimps, he remains fundamentally disconnected.

three decades: thirty years

wretched: horrible

keepers: zoo workers

mating: procreating; pairing for the purpose of breeding

catch your breath: stop for a moment when something surprises or shocks you

twist: turn

4 Watching Herman in his cage, stamping back and forth, it becomes easy to understand the ambivalence so many people feel toward zoos. When I consider his life in this enclosure, so far from where he belongs, I feel a sense of loss.

5 But seeing Herman is marvellous, too. If you stand in front of the exhibit and meet his gaze when he is calm, a glimmer of recognition sparks between you. The reality of him—as he scratches his head and studies you in return—makes you catch your breath.

6 The same conflicting reactions twist inside you as you walk through the rest of the zoo, seeing all the animals collected inside these walls. Pleasure is weighted with guilt. All zoos, even the most enlightened, are built upon an idea that is fascinating and repulsive—the notion that we can seek out the wildness of the world and view its beauty, but that we must first contain that wildness.

7 Zoos argue that they are fighting for the conservation of the Earth, that they educate the public and provide refuge and support for vanishing species. And they are right.

8 Animal rights groups argue that zoos traffic in living creatures, exploiting them for financial gain and amusement. And they are right.

unease: anxiety or discomfort

9 Caught inside this contradiction are the animals themselves and the humans charged with their well-being. At Lowry Park, the keepers love animals and are deeply attached to the ones in their care. But their attachment does not blind them to the moral complexities of what they do. After it was announced that Lowry Park and San Diego were purchasing eleven elephants from Swaziland, many keepers reacted with quiet unease. The difficulties of caring for elephants are well known in zoo circles. No institution has imported African elephants into the United States in more than ten years.

10 At Lowry Park, the staff heard the official rationale for buying the elephants: the overcrowding in the Swazi game parks and the fact that the elephants were going to be killed. Yet for all the altruistic talk of rescuing these animals, there is no question that Lowry Park is gaining a desirable prize in return. Already the zoo is constructing a huge new African section to showcase the elephants.

prize: valuable reward or gift (do not confuse with price, which means "cost")

11 We think of Africa as a continent of vast, unclaimed spaces, where species can roam to the horizon. In reality, humans occupy so much of the continent that many animals are confined inside game parks. Although these parks are often huge by our standards—sometimes stretching across hundreds of miles—the animals increasingly find their movement restricted by human boundaries and human priorities.

paves over: covers with roads, parking lots, etc.

12 As our species paves over the planet, we seek consolation in the myth of unlimited freedom. We watch *The Lion King* with our kids, singing along as Simba and Pumba majestically celebrate the circle of life. But the truth is, the circle of life is constantly shrinking. If you are going to see a lion, even in Africa, it will almost certainly be on a tour inside a fenced park.

fenced: enclosed with a barrier

(738 words)

Source: French, Thomas. "Zoo Story: The New World." *St. Petersburg Times.* 2 Dec 2007. Web.

"Zoo Story" is a challenging reading for students. There are additional questions on the Companion Website. Students can check their scores with the automated grading function.

VOCABULARY AND COMPREHENSION

1 In paragraph 5, the writer says, "If you stand in front of the exhibit and meet his gaze when he is calm, a glimmer of recognition sparks between you." What does this mean?

   a. When your eyes meet Herman's eyes, you realize that you are not so different from each other.

   b. When Herman is calm, he can remember who you are.

2 Find one word in paragraph 11 that means "walk freely over large distances."

   Roam

3 Find one word in paragraph 12 that means "getting smaller."

Shrinking

4 Where was Herman born? ___Africa___

5 What is Herman's identity crisis? ___He thinks he is a human.___

6 Why does Herman believe he is a human?

a. He is in a zoo and people watch him every day.

(b.) When he was small, a human family raised him and treated him like a child.

c. He never sees other chimpanzees.

7 What is the writer's opinion of zoos?

a. Zoos educate the public and help save endangered species.

b. Zoos exploit animals to make money and to provide entertainment.

(c.) Both a and b

8 Lowry Park is buying more elephants. Why do the elephants have to leave Africa?

The game park is overcrowded and the animals will be killed.

9 In paragraphs 11 and 12, what point is the writer making about Africa?

Even in Africa, animals cannot run freely. They are in fenced parks.

Writing topics related to "Zoo Story" appear in the Take Action! section.

WRITE QUESTIONS

10 Imagine that you could meet the author of this text, Thomas French. Write five questions for him.

1. _____

_____

_____

2. _____

_____

_____

3. _____

_____

_____

4. _____

_____

_____

5. _____

_____

_____

Take Action!

© PEARSON LONGMAN • REPRODUCTION PROHIBITED

These topics can be used as individual and team writing or speaking tests. For additional topics, visit the Teacher Section of the Companion Website. Then click on "Writing" or "Speaking."

WRITING TOPICS

Write about one of the following topics. For information about paragraph and essay structure, see the Writing Workshops on pages 127-140.

1 Vegetarian or Meat Eater?

In a paragraph of about 100 words, defend your decision to eat meat or to be a vegetarian.

2 Natural World

The book and movie *Into the Wild* explore a young man's decision to live alone in the wild. Write two paragraphs describing your experiences with the natural world.

- First, describe your preferences. What do you like best: a beach, a forest, or a mountain? Explain why. Near your home, what place in nature do you enjoy? What do you do there?
- Then write about a place in nature that you loved when you were a child. Where did you go? What did you do there?

3 Zoos

Read "Zoo Story." Describe any experiences you have had in the past with wild animals. Did you visit a zoo or animal safari park? Did you encounter animals in the wild? In a paragraph, describe what happened.

SPEAKING TOPICS

Prepare a presentation about one of the following topics.

1 Pet Ownership Rules

Before someone buys a dog or cat, what do they need to know? What do pets require? Explain what pet owners should do. Discuss feeding, walking, training, and so on. You can also discuss the cost of owning a pet.

2 Opinions about Pets

In some cultures, people do not keep domestic animals. Cats are considered vermin, and they live in the streets. What is your opinion about domestic animals? Are they useful or are they a waste of money? Provide specific examples from your life or the lives of people you know.

- If you believe pets are useful, show ways that pets help humans.
- If you think pets are not useful, give your reasons.

3 Experience in Nature

Describe a good or a bad experience that you had in nature. Where did you go? What happened? Why was it a good or bad experience?

SPEAKING PRESENTATION TIPS

- PRACTISE YOUR PRESENTATION and time yourself. You should speak for about two minutes.
- USE CUE CARDS. DO NOT READ! Put about fifteen words on your cue cards.
- BRING VISUAL SUPPORT, such as a picture, photograph, object, video, or PowerPoint slides.
- CLASSMATES WILL ASK YOU QUESTIONS about your presentation. You must also ask classmates about their presentations. Review how to form questions before your presentation day.

VOCABULARY REVIEW

Review key terms from this chapter. Identify the words you do not understand and learn what they mean.

- ☐ calf
- ☐ fence
- ☐ grief
- ☐ hind legs
- ☐ hunt
- ☐ nest
- ☐ poisonous
- ☐ rescue
- ☐ trap
- ☐ tusk
- ☐ wet
- ☐ woods

COMPANION web+ To practise vocabulary from this chapter, visit the Companion Website.

Revising and Editing

The Revising and Editing sections at the end of each chapter help your students prepare for writing tests, including Benchmark and TESOL tests. Students can do the activities with a partner and share ideas.

REVISE FOR SUPPORTING DETAILS

A good paragraph should include supporting details. Practise revising a student paragraph. Add examples to make the paragraph more complete. (To learn more about paragraph and essay writing, see the Writing Workshops on pages 127-140.)

Animals help us in our lives. First, dogs are useful in many ways. _____

_____

_____

Of course, animals provide us with food. _____

_____

_____

Finally, some animals are beautiful to look at. _____

_____

_____

We should appreciate the creatures that share our planet.

EDIT PAST TENSE VERBS

Practise editing a student paragraph. Underline and correct six verb tense errors. The first one is done for you as an example.

                                            had

When I was a child, I loved nature. My stepfather ~~haved~~ a cottage, and

                                                   were

we went there in the summers and during vacations. My brother and I <u>was</u>

                                 need   **did**

really busy at that cottage. We didn't <u>needed</u> a television. What we do? We

                                      swam   **built**

cut firewood. We played board games. We <u>swum</u> in the lake, and we <u>builded</u>

a fort in the trees. We often saw wild animals like deer and skunks. Also,

      took

we <u>taked</u> our dog for walks every night, even if it was cold outside. Later,

when my stepfather sold the cottage, I lost my favourite place in nature.

Grammar TIP

Was or Were

In the past tense, use **was** when the subject is *I*, *he*, *she*, or *it*. Use **were** when the subject is *you*, *we*, or *they*.

    were

We ~~was~~ busy when we stayed at the cottage.

To learn more about past tense verbs, see Unit 4 in *Avenues 1: English Grammar*.

"When you travel, remember that a foreign country is not designed to make you comfortable. It is designed to make its own people comfortable."

– CLIFTON FADIMAN

CHAPTER 5

Travel and Cultural Traditions

Why do people travel? What are the benefits of learning about other cultural traditions? In this chapter, you will read about travelling and cultural traditions.

START UP

Make the Start Up into a timed competition. Place students in teams and give them about three minutes to guess as many answers as they can.

Name That Country

Work with a team of students. View the list of cities. Then indicate the names of the countries where these cities are located. Also write the nationalities. If you are not sure, you can guess.

Cities	Country	Nationality
EXAMPLE: *Paris, Lyon, Marseilles*	*France*	*French*
1 Madrid, Barcelona, Seville	Spain	Spanish
2 Zurich, Geneva, Lausanne	Switzerland	Swiss
3 Athens, Sparta, Naxos	Greece	Greek
4 Johannesburg, Capetown, Mbombela	South Africa	South African
5 Sydney, Brisbane, Melbourne	Australia	Australian
6 Chicago, Dallas, Seattle	USA	American
7 Frankfurt, Hamburg, Berlin	Germany	German
8 Edinburgh, Glasgow, Aberdeen	Scotland	Scottish
9 Moscow, St. Petersburg, Ufa	Russia	Russian
10 Dublin, Cork, Galway	Ireland	Irish
11 Vancouver, Toronto, Montreal	Canada	Canadian
12 Rio de Janeiro, Brasilia, São Paulo	Brazil	Brazilian
13 Delhi, Mumbai, Madras	India	Indian
14 Acapulco, Cancun, Tijuana	Mexico	Mexican
15 Beijing, Shanghai, Guangzhou	China	Chinese

Moscow

Capetown

Edinburgh

Grammar
TIP

Using *The*

Do not put *the* before most city and country names. Some exceptions are *the United States* and *the Dominican Republic*.

I visited Brazil, China, Australia, and Ireland.

To learn more about articles, see Unit 5 in *Avenues 1: English Grammar*.

You can ask students to do Reading 5.1 together in class, and then assign Readings 5.2 and 5.3 as homework. Or you can divide students into teams and treat this as a jigsaw activity. Different groups read either Reading 5.1, Reading 5.2, or Reading 5.3. Then the teams can regroup, explain what they have read, and share their answers.

Gestures and gift-giving rules differ around the world. Read about some rules that are common in Asia.

GRAMMAR LINK

When you come to parentheses in the text, underline the correct verb forms. On the Companion Website, you can listen to this essay and check your answers.

Giving Gifts in Asia

As students read this text, they also practise verb tenses. It is a good review of present, past, and future verbs, and modals. Students can check their answers in class or by listening to the reading on the Companion Website.

BY C. WINLAND

1 I am a business traveller, and I visit nations around the world. I discovered that every nation has particular gift-giving rules.

2 One of the most interesting nations is Singapore. The government has very effective anti-corruption legislation and prides itself on being one of the most corruption-free countries in the world. In Singapore, government employees cannot accept gifts. The police (<u>will arrest</u> / will arresting) public officials, including government ministers, who accept a bribe.

3 In Singapore, if you want to thank somebody in an office, you (<u>must give</u> / must to give) a gift to everyone. During a 2009 business trip, I wanted to thank a receptionist for her help and hospitality. I (have to gave / <u>had to give</u>) a gift to the entire department. The group graciously accepted my gift.

4 To be polite, most individuals in Singapore and Malaysia will initially refuse a gift. If you continue to insist, the recipients will accept the gift. However, they (<u>won't unwrap</u> / won't unwrapping) it in front of you because it implies that they are impatient and greedy. Instead, they will thank you and then wait to open the gift in private.

5 You also have to consider the type of gift you give. In Singapore and Malaysia, never give a gift that is sharp or that cuts because it symbolizes cutting the relationship. So you (<u>shouldn't buy</u> / shouldn't to buy) a set of knives for your hostess. In Muslim countries, or when you visit a family of practising Muslims, do not bring wine to a meal. The *Koran* forbids alcohol, so it's a good idea to assume that your hosts (<u>don't drink</u> / doesn't drink). You should even avoid gifts that contain alcohol, such as perfume. In China, you (must not to give / <u>must not give</u>) gifts that are in white or green wrapping paper because those colours are unlucky. In Japan, the number four sounds like the word meaning "death," so most people (won't giving / <u>won't give</u>) gifts that contain four items.

6 Finally, in Japan, if someone (give / <u>gives</u>) you a business card, treat his or her gesture with respect. It is rude to put the card in your pocket immediately. Instead, take the time to read the card. With a nod, acknowledge that you read it. Then you (<u>can put</u> / can putting) it in your pocket.

7 To avoid insulting their hosts, business travellers need to know about gift-giving customs in other nations.

(403 words)

Sources: "Cultural Competence for Professional Travel in Singapore." Illinois International. Web.
"Singapore Gift Giving Customs." Giftpedia. Web.

COMPREHENSION

1 In paragraph 2, what is a *bribe*?

A gift given to influence or corrupt someone

2 In paragraph 4, what is the meaning of *unwrap*? (Circle the letter of the correct answer.)

a. Open a gift (remove packaging)   b. Accept a gift   c. Look at

3 Find a word in paragraph 5 that means "prohibits; does not permit."

Forbids

4 Find a word in paragraph 6 that means "not polite."

Rude

5 You presented a gift to a business associate in Singapore. He refused to accept the gift three times. What should you do?

a. Keep insisting. He may take it the fourth time.

b. Apologize for offering the gift, and then take it home.

c. Show understanding and offer the gift to his secretary instead. She will open it.

6 You bought this gift for your hostess in Japan. Now she is offended. What mistake did you make?

a. The word for *four* sounds like "death" in Japanese, and you brought four flowers.

b. Flowers are from the soil and are insulting in Japan.

c. In Japanese, a flower means "love," and your hostess is married.

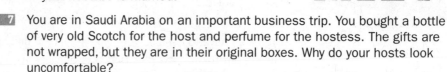

7 You are in Saudi Arabia on an important business trip. You bought a bottle of very old Scotch for the host and perfume for the hostess. The gifts are not wrapped, but they are in their original boxes. Why do your hosts look uncomfortable?

a. Gifts containing alcohol, even perfume, are not appropriate in Muslim countries.

b. Your gifts are considered a bribe, so you insulted your hosts.

c. You did not wrap the gifts. Unwrapped gifts suggest that you have no respect for the hosts.

8 You are in Japan, and this man is offering you a business card. What should you do?

a. Examine the card carefully to show that you are reading it. Then put it in your pocket.

b. Politely refuse to accept the card.

c. Immediately put the card in your wallet.

9 What is the principal idea of this essay?

Travellers should learn about gift-giving rules in other countries.

When you travel, innocent movements and gestures can have unintended meanings. Read about some not-so-innocent gestures.

Not-So-Innocent Gestures

BY VIGGO ULLMAN

1 We often think that gestures and expressions are the same all over the world. But gestures can mean different things in different places. For instance, while most people in the world nod their heads up and down to indicate "yes," in Turkey and Greece an upward nod means "no." A head movement to the side means "yes" in that region of the world. This subtle difference can be rather confusing for tourists.

2 When I strapped on my backpack and travelled, I made some stupid mistakes. In Russia, I offended a cute woman who I wanted to impress. We were in a bus, and I made eye contact with her. Then, without thinking, I winked at her. When the bus stopped, I followed her out and tried to talk with her. When I asked her if she spoke English, she gave me a really angry look, and she quickly walked away. Later, a Russian man explained that when you wink at a Russian woman, it means that you are calling her a prostitute.

3 I also managed to offend someone in India. While I was travelling in a train from Delhi to Agra, I crossed my legs. The man across from me looked very upset. Then he lectured me and said that my action was very rude. He explained that I should never show the sole of my shoe to someone. The gesture meant that I consider the person to be lower than the bottom of my foot. After that, I was careful to keep my feet on the floor. Also, in India, you must not pat a child on the head. The head, which is the highest part of the body, is considered sacred.

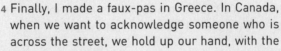

4 Finally, I made a faux-pas in Greece. In Canada, when we want to acknowledge someone who is across the street, we hold up our hand, with the fingers slightly spread, and we wave. Our palm faces out. But in Greece, if you show your five fingers like that, you will curse a person's family for five generations. So, when you are in a store and you want to buy five items, or if you just want to wave at someone, turn your palm toward yourself. Or even better, just keep your fingers together and don't spread them.

5 Many other gestures can be misinterpreted. The thumbs up gesture is an obscene insult in the Middle East and Bangladesh. When you make the okay sign, you can offend people in parts of South America. If you are planning to travel extensively, take the time to learn about gestures in other countries.

(436 words)

Additional questions for this essay appear on the Companion Website. You can verify if students have read the essay by checking their scores with the grade tracker.

COMPREHENSION

1 In paragraph 1, what is the meaning of *nod*?
   a. incline   b. close   c. neck

2 Find a verb in paragraph 2 that means "closed and opened one eye quickly." (See the photo.)

   Winked

3 In paragraph 2, why was the Russian woman offended?

If you wink at a Russian woman, you are calling her a prostitute.

4 In paragraph 3, what does *pat* mean?

(a.) Touch lightly　　　b. A woman's name　　　c. Walk

5 In paragraph 4, what does *curse* mean?

a. Say a bad word

b. Write

(c.) Wish to invoke bad fortune on someone

6 The man with the striped shirt is in India. What mistake is he making?

a. He is wearing sunglasses.

(b.) He is pointing the bottom of his foot toward someone.

c. He is dressed too casually.

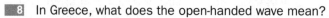

7 Why should you never pat a child on the head in India?

The head is considered sacred.

8 In Greece, what does the open-handed wave mean?

a. Hello or goodbye

b. Please go away.

(c.) I inflict bad luck on your family for five generations.

9 What is the principal idea of this essay?

Gestures have different meanings in different in countries around the world.

📖 READING 5.3

What should you do in a Japanese bath? In a letter, a young traveller describes his adventures in a Japanese bathhouse.

The Japanese Bath

BY ANTHONY WADE

1 My most interesting experience in Japan was in a traditional Japanese bathhouse, which is called a *sento*. In the past, both men and women had public baths together, but today the genders bathe separately. There is one section for males and another for females.

2 I visited a public bath in Osaka. I didn't know the rules, so I copied the other men's actions. In a small room, I took off all of my clothing. Then I entered another room that was filled with men sitting on small stools. Everyone turned to look at me because I was a foreigner. But then the men ignored me and continued to clean themselves.

3 I sat on the stool like the others. I used soap and a cloth to scrub myself. The other men were taking a long time to scrub, so I washed my face and body thoroughly. I spent fifteen minutes scrubbing my body and shampooing my hair. Then after I was very clean, I grabbed a bucket. I scooped some water out of a hot tub. I poured the water over myself and rinsed off the dirt and soap. I did exactly what the Japanese men were doing.

4 In Japan, you must be completely clean *before* you enter the bathtub. You can't bring soap or shampoo into the tub. The tubs were quite large, and two or three men were in each tub, talking quietly. I climbed into a tub with a Japanese man. The water was extremely hot.

5 While I was soaking in the hot water, a naked Australian tourist entered the room, and we introduced ourselves. His name was Kenny, and he climbed directly into my hot tub. He didn't wash his body first, so he was dirty. He brought soap into the tub with him. Everyone else stared at him, shocked.

6 He and I were the only ones who spoke English. I whispered to Kenny that he shouldn't bring soap into the tub. I talked about the sento rules and explained that he should wash himself first and then come into the tub. I also told him that he was upsetting the others. But he just laughed and said, "Who cares, mate?" Kenny had long blond hair. He leaned over and wet his hair. Then he rubbed it with soap. He rinsed out his hair in the hot tub water. The Japanese man and I had to sit in Kenny's soapy water.

7 Kenny was not embarrassed. He ignored the angry looks of the other men. Then Kenny complained about the local people. His loud voice really echoed in the room. The other men in the room looked at Kenny and shook their heads with disgust. I had to agree with the Japanese men. Kenny was acting like a rude and disrespectful foreigner.

(465 words)

VOCABULARY AND COMPREHENSION

1 Match the photos with the correct terms from the list below. Look at the words in context before you write your answers. The paragraph numbers are in parentheses.

stool (3) scrub (3) pour (3) soak (5)

1. _____ pour _____

(immerse in warm water)

2. _____ soak _____

3. _____ scrub _____

4. _____ stool _____

2 Find a verb in paragraph 6 that means "spoke quietly." _____ Whispered _____

3 In paragraph 7, what is the meaning of *rude*?

a. friendly   (b.) inconsiderate; impolite   c. severe

4 What are the steps you should follow when you enter a Japanese sento? Number the steps in order.

2 Scrub your body with a cloth and soap

4 Soak in a hot tub

5 Put on your clothes

1 Take off your clothes

3 Rinse off the soap

5 What mistakes did Kenny, the Australian tourist, make? Name at least two things.

He brought soap into the bathtub. He talked loudly in the bathhouse.

6 What was the writer's opinion of Kenny?

He was rude and disrespectful.

7 What is the writer's message?

(a.) When you are the guest in another country, respect that country's values and traditions.

b. When you are in another country, visit the local attractions.

WRITING

With a partner, discuss what travellers should and should not do. To get ideas, think about some of the mistakes that travellers made in Readings 5.1, 5.2, and 5.3. Then create a list of suggestions for travellers.

Grammar
TIP

Using *Should*

When you give advice, you can use the modal auxiliary *should*.

Always use the base form of the verb after *should*.

bring
A traveller should not ~~brings~~ too many books.

To learn more about modals such as *should*, see Unit 9 In *Avenues 1: English Grammar.*

Vocabulary
BOOST

Travel Terms

Do not confuse some travel-related terms.

Travel is usually used as a verb. You *travel* to another place.

Trip is a noun. You take a *trip* somewhere.

    noun   *verb*

I took a **trip** to Jamaica. I **travelled** to Jamaica.

PRACTICE

Practise using more travel words. Write the letters of the best definitions in the spaces provided.

Terms		Definitions
1. round-trip ticket	c	a. enter; get on
2. vacancy	e	b. holiday
3. vacation	b	c. ticket to a destination and back home
4. book (a ticket)	f	d. dividing line between two countries
5. border	d	e. available space in a hotel or motel
6. board (a plane)	a	f. reserve

The Chapter Review exercise on the Companion Website offers more practice using travel-related vocabulary.

💬 **SPEAKING** # Travel Experiences

Work with a partner and discuss how to form the following questions. First, choose the correct auxiliary verbs from the list below and use each item once. Then ask your partner the questions. Write your partner's answers on the lines.

    did   do   should   was   will

Partner's name: _____

1. What _____do_____ you do every year during your summer vacation?

   Answer: _____

   _____

2. Where _____did_____ you travel when you were a child?

   Answer: _____

   _____

3. What _____was_____ your favourite destination when you were a child?

   Answer: _____

   _____

4. In the future, where _____will_____ you travel? Explain why.

   Answer: _____

   _____

5. What _____should_____ people bring with them when they travel? List at least five things.

   Answer: _____

   _____

   _____

WRITING

Write a paragraph about your partner. Include your partner's answers to the questions.

◀)) **LISTENING PRACTICE**

The listening segments are included in the Companion Website. You can assign the listening activities in class or give them as homework.

1. Listen to Travel Plans

Listen to Reena's travel plans. Fill in the missing information.

1. First name: Reena   Last name: ___Jindal___

2. Age: Twenty-four

3. Duration of her trip (Choose one answer.)

   a. Two weeks   (b.) Two months   c. Six months

4. Departure date: June 12

5. Airline for her trip to Beijing: Air Canada

6. Cost of flight to Beijing: $970

7. Length of flight to Beijing: Thirteen hours

8. Departure time: 1:15 p.m.

9. Arrival time: June 13th   2:00 p.m.

10. What countries will she visit? Number the destinations in order.

    __6__ India   __3__ Thailand   __1__ China

    __2__ South Korea   __5__ Singapore   __4__ Malaysia

2. Follow Directions

Josh Holton is in the city of Glasgow, Scotland. Today he is visiting the city. Follow his journey. Begin on the "Start" circle. Then follow his path, and write the following places on the map.

bakery   bank   barber   cinema   gallery   hospital

Before you listen, review the following vocabulary.

- **block** a rectangular section of a city enclosed by streets; the area between two streets
- **straight ahead** ↑
- **turn right** ↱
- **turn left** ↰

🔊 LISTENING Traditions in Somalia

Mawlid Abdoul-Aziz left Somalia and came to Canada. Mawlid discusses some of Somalia's cultural traditions.

PRE-LISTENING VOCABULARY

Match the following words with the correct definitions. Write the letters of the definitions in the spaces provided.

Terms

1. feast ___d___
2. fast ___e___
3. sunset ___c___
4. donate ___a___
5. sick ___b___

Definitions

a. give to a charity or person in need

b. ill; not healthy

c. disappearance of the sun below the horizon

d. special meal or banquet

e. abstain from eating or drinking

COMPREHENSION

1 In Somalia, what is the family name?

a. It is the father's last name.

b. It is the name of the tribe.

c. It is the first names of many male ancestors. *(circled)*

2 How many names did Mawlid have to memorize?

a. three

b. fifteen

c. twenty-three *(circled)*

Market in Hargeisa, Somalia

3 What does Mawlid do during Ramadan? Name two things.

He cannot eat or drink during the day. He must give money to the poor.

4 Usually, at what age do people begin fasting for Ramadan?

a. eight   b. fifteen *(circled)*   c. eighteen

5 At what age did Mawlid first begin the practice of fasting for Ramadan?

a. eight *(circled)*   b. fifteen   c. eighteen

6 For Mawlid, what is the most difficult part of Ramadan?

Going without water

7 What happens at the end of Ramadan?

People have a large meal and exchange gifts.

Indicate if the following sentences are true or false. Circle T for "true" or F for "false."

8 In Somalia, girls must memorize the names of their male ancestors.   (T)   F

9 Muslims celebrate Ramadan every September.   T   (F)

10 People in Somalia have special celebrations for birthdays.   T   (F)

READING STRATEGY

Students can visit the Companion Website to practise reading strategies. Exercises about main idea, context clues, etc., are structured to help students do better in their reading tests, including Benchmark and TESOL tests.

You can prepare for your reading tests by visiting the Companion Website. Click on "Reading Strategies" to find a variety of practice exercises.

Identifying the Thesis and Topic Sentences

The main idea is the principal focus of a text. It may be expressed in the title, introduction, or conclusion. Look for a **thesis statement**, which is a sentence that expresses the main idea. The thesis is usually at the end of an introductory paragraph.

An essay is supported with facts and examples. Often, each body paragraph has a **topic sentence**. The topic sentence supports the thesis and expresses the main idea of the paragraph.

Sometimes writers do not write thesis statements or topic sentences. If you cannot find a statement with the main idea, then ask yourself *who*, *what*, *when*, *where*, *why*, and *how* questions. In one or two sentences, you can write your own statement of the main idea.

READING 5.4

In every society, there are ceremonies to celebrate the loving union of a couple. Read about the history and varieties of wedding ceremonies. After you finish reading the text, you will be asked to define the words in green.

Wedding Traditions

BY D. PELAEZ

killer: fabulous; great

common-law: cohabiting without marriage

1 A friend of mine is getting married next Saturday, and I am the best man. I found a rented tux, and I plan to enjoy myself at a killer party. Still, I wondered why he's getting married. Here in Quebec, weddings are becoming irrelevant. A recent survey showed that almost 40 percent of Quebec couples are in common-law relationships. So is marriage an **outdated** institution? Because I have a part to play in a "white wedding," I decided to investigate the ritual. Weddings have a fascinating history and a great variety of traditions.

2 In a white wedding, the **bride** and **groom** marry in a church or temple and exchange exchange **vows** and wedding rings. Certain white wedding traditions—the bride dresses in a long white **gown**, carries flowers, and has at least one bridesmaid—have both practical and supernatural sources. Originally, white symbolized "purity" because the bride was expected to be a virgin. Also, in past centuries, the bride carried flowers to mask body odour because people rarely bathed. Imagine if you suggested that a bride carry flowers for that reason now! Do you know why bridesmaids have to buy those embarrassing gowns? In previous eras, people believed that evil spirits would take away the bride. If bridesmaids also wore long gowns, the spirits would get confused and not recognize the bride. Apparently, evil spirits don't have very good vision.

3 Throughout most of human history, a wedding was a business deal. The wife was considered the husband's property. Often, the bride's parents had to give money to the groom's family. In many cultures, the groom and the "**best man**" would kidnap the bride and force her to become a member of the groom's tribe. Luckily, all the best man has to do these days is give a speech full of embarrassing anecdotes about the groom.

4 The white wedding ceremony exists in many cultures, but details about the ceremony differ. Mexican Catholics place a lasso—usually a white rope—around the necks of the bride and groom to symbolize their unity. In Jewish weddings, the groom stomps on a glass at the end of the ceremony, and the broken glass symbolizes a marriage that will last for as long as the glass is broken: forever.

© PEARSON LONGMAN • REPRODUCTION PROHIBITED

frat: fraternity (universities have fraternities where male students live)

smash: break into pieces

present: something given; a gift

widows: the wives of men who died

handkerchief: a small piece of cloth

5 Some wedding traditions are silly rather than serious and would be more appropriate at a frat party. In Scotland, there is a pre-wedding tradition called "Blackening of the Bride." The bride is covered with eggs, sauces, and feathers, and then paraded around town. It is supposed to be fun ... for the **guests**, at least. In some American wedding receptions, the groom shoves cake into the bride's face. It is supposed to be funny, but I'm sure the bride doesn't laugh. In Germany, it is considered good luck for all the guests of the wedding to smash old dishes on the floor. The bride and the groom then have to gather all the pieces to show the strength of their union. Everyone always has a lot of fun doing this, but it sounds like a poor wedding present.

6 Think of all the time women spend here shopping for a wedding dress. Imagine if they had to find three! In a traditional Japanese wedding, the bride changes three times. First, the bride's face and hands are painted white, and she wears a traditional Japanese kimono. The bride and groom drink sake—a type of rice-wine—in front of the priest. Then the bride changes into a more conventional wedding gown to celebrate with the guests. She changes for a third time to participate in a candle ceremony.

7 Not all weddings are white. In many African countries, the bride chooses any colour that she likes for the wedding, and everybody comes dressed in the same colour. My sister, who works in the Congo, had to buy an orange outfit for an orange wedding. In some Asian countries, red is the colour of marriage. In India, brides wear long red saris. In fact, white symbolizes death, and only widows dress completely in white. In China, red symbolizes luck and good fortune. Red is everywhere in a Chinese wedding— the table-settings are red and the flowers are red. Even the homes of the bride and groom are completely decorated in red. Also, the bride and groom give each other a red handkerchief with a picture of a pair of ducks. Ducks are considered monogamous birds, which is why they are a Chinese symbol for a long marriage. In reality, ducks only stay with the same **mate** for about a year or two. Maybe they are a better symbol for modern marriage?

8 Personally, I don't plan on getting married. The expense and ceremony don't appeal to me. I believe common-law unions make more sense in a modern context. Still, I understand the value of family and community bonding over the marriage of a couple. I'm pleased that same-sex marriage is gaining acceptance. And any event that involves a seven-course meal can't be all that bad.

(832 words)

Sources: Jacks, Matt. "The History of Weddings." *The Wedding Zone*. Net Guides Publishing Inc. 2004. Web. "German Wedding Traditions." *World Wedding Traditions*. Euroevents and Travel. 2004. Web. "Wedding Customs Around the World." *Topics Online Magazine*. Topics Online Magazine. 2005. Web.

On the Companion Website, there are additional vocabulary and comprehension questions for "Wedding Traditions." The questions can serve as a practice test or as a formal reading test.

VOCABULARY AND COMPREHENSION

1 Define the following words. Use context clues to help you. The paragraph numbers are in parentheses, and in the essay, the words appear in green. Use a dictionary only if necessary.

1. outdated (1): out of date; not common anymore

2. bride (2): woman who will get married

3. groom (2): man who will get married

4. vows (2): solemn promises

5. gown (2): long dress

6. best man (3): man who helps the groom at a wedding

7. guests (5): invited friends or members of the family

8. mate (7): partner; companion

2 Look at paragraph 1. Highlight a sentence that sums up the principal idea of the essay. (That sentence is called a thesis statement.)

3 Underline the topic sentence in paragraphs 2 to 7. The topic sentence sums up the principal idea of the paragraph. Be careful because the topic sentence is not always the first sentence in the paragraph.

WRITING

In a paragraph of about 120 words, give your opinion about marriage. When two people love each other, should they marry or should they live common-law?

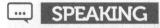

Holidays and Celebrations

In each question, underline the correct auxiliary verb. Then ask your partner the questions. Write your partner's answers on the lines provided.

EXAMPLE: What (*is* / *are*) your name? _____ *Isabelle* _____

Partner's name: _____

1 In your culture, what (is / <u>are</u>) the most important holidays and celebrations?

Holidays	**Celebrations**
(religious, ethnic, seasonal, or national holidays and festivals)	(stage of life celebrations)
EXAMPLE: *Valentine's Day*	EXAMPLE: *birthday*
April Fool's Day, Canada Day, Mother's Day,	Baby shower, wedding, funeral, baptism,
New Year's Eve, Labour Day, Boxing Day,	coming of age ceremony such as a
religious holidays, etc.	bar mitzvah, etc.

2 Which holiday during the year (<u>do you</u> / are you) prefer?

_____

On that holiday, who do you spend time with?

_____

_____

3 What (do you did / <u>did you do</u>) on your favourite holiday last year? Describe at least four things that you did.

_____

_____

_____

_____

_____

_____

An essay topic related to this speaking activity appears in the Take Action! section on page 85.

4 In the future, how (you will / <u>will you</u>) celebrate your favourite holiday?

_____

_____

_____

_____

5 Why (do / <u>does</u>) every culture have special holidays and celebrations? List at least three reasons.

Possible answers: to celebrate a life passage such as birth, marriage, or death

– to remember a political or religious event

– to honour a great person

– to bring the family together

_____

WRITING

In a paragraph of about 120 words, write about a holiday or celebration that is significant to your partner.

Rethinking Bullfights

The first Spanish bullfight took place about three hundred years ago. Since then, bullfighting has been a strong cultural tradition in Spain. But these days, there is a growing movement to end the sport. Watch the video about Spain's cultural tradition of bullfighting.

VOCABULARY

1 Fill in the blanks with one of the following words:

always	families	what	how long
beauty	injuries	who	where

For first-timers, Las Ventas Bullfighting plaza in Madrid can initially be a place of delicate _____beauty_____, of dazzling colours and entire _____families_____ on a night out. It is a performance they come to see, and a performance they _____always_____ get. Ultimately, it's a drama.

That's the point of the whole endeavour. Three matadors, six bulls.

_____ better to describe this than a bullfighting reviewer who has seen so much? There is truth in the bullring, he says. It's not theatre or cinema, _____ there are ways to cheat, and where there are rehearsals. There is mystery in _____ happens to the matadors. Sometimes, as in this night, _____ can be serious: a broken jaw, a concussion. But for the bulls, the only uncertainty seems _____ it will take to die.

COMPREHENSION AND WRITING

2 Write two paragraphs about the video. Each paragraph should be about 70 to 100 words long.

In the first paragraph, summarize the content of the video. Include the following information.
- Who supports the bullfighting ban? Why do they support it?
- Who is against the bullfighting ban? Why are they against it?

In your second paragraph, give your opinion. Bullfighting is a cultural tradition in Spain. Should the government ban it? Why or why not?

SPEAKING

Sports and Culture

Ask a partner the following questions. Write your partner's answers on the lines provided.

1 What are the most important sports and games in your region? Rank the top five sports in order of popularity.

1. _____
2. _____
3. _____
4. _____
5. _____

2 What are some positive and negative points about the most popular sport?

Positive points	Negative points
_____	_____
_____	_____
_____	_____
_____	_____

3 Think of a specific time when your country's sport unified the nation. What happened?

_____

_____

_____

4 In the past, what actions reflected badly on your country's sport? Did the public riot or behave badly? Did players behave badly? Think of an event.

_____

_____

_____

5 Why do people in every culture have sports and games? Think of at least two reasons.

Possible answers: To unite people / To showcase exceptional talent / To have fun

_____

_____

Have a class discussion about the reasons societies have sports and games. Possible reasons are to provide an outlet for aggression, to keep people physically fit, to provide friendly competition, and to make a group feel united (with their team).

WRITING

Write a short essay about <u>one</u> of the following topics.

1 Explain why every culture has team sports. Then in a second paragraph, describe sports that you participated in during your childhood.

2 Describe your country's national sport. What are some positive and negative aspects of the sport? Give specific examples of positive or negative moments during that sport. Then in a second paragraph, explain why every society has team sports.

Take Action!

On the Companion Website, you can find evaluation grids and additional speaking and writing topics.

These writing topics can also be used as speaking topics.

WRITING TOPICS

Write about one of the following topics. For information about essay structure, see Writing Workshop 2 on page 131.

1 Family History

Describe your family's history.

- Where did your family originate? How did your family get here?
- How is your family's native country different from this country?

2 Travelling

Write an essay about travelling.

- First, explain why people travel. What can they learn when they visit other places?
- Then describe a trip that you took when you were younger. Where did you go? What did you do?
- Finally, describe a place you would like to visit in the future. Explain why you would like to go there.

3 Holidays and Traditions

Write about holidays and traditions.

· First, explain why people in all cultures have special holidays and traditions.

· Then describe a past holiday or celebration that you enjoyed. What happened?

· What will you celebrate in the future? What will you do?

SPEAKING TOPICS

Speaking Topic 1 can be a team presentation. Each student works individually on his or her part of the presentation.

1 Local Tourism

Make a video or a PowerPoint presentation. Choose one of the following topics. Your audience is people from other countries.

a. Describe a cultural holiday or celebration that is popular in your region. How do people prepare for the event?

b. Promote your town or city to tourists. Explain why people should visit it. What can they do? Discuss specific attractions in your area.

c. Describe a certain type of cuisine that is popular in your region. Explain how to make the food or describe the best place to find the food.

d. Give advice for visitors who are coming to your area. What should they pack? What is the weather like? What information do travellers need if they are coming to your region?

e. Describe a traditional, unusual, or new sport or game that is popular in your region. Briefly give important features of the sport. Remember that your audience is not familiar with the sport.

2 Travel Project

Talk about a place that you visited or you would like to visit. Present some basic information about that place. Your presentation should include most of the following information.

Location: Explain where the place is located.

Cost: What is the best price for plane tickets to that location?

Currency: What kind of currency will people need? What is the exchange rate?

Accommodations: Where can a student stay? Do some research online to find inexpensive accommodations.

Attractions: Describe some things that visitors can do in that place.

VOCABULARY REVIEW

Review key terms from this chapter. Identify the words you do not understand and learn what they mean.

- ☐ book (a trip)
- ☐ border
- ☐ gift
- ☐ guest
- ☐ nod
- ☐ pour
- ☐ travel
- ☐ trip
- ☐ vacancy
- ☐ vacation
- ☐ wave
- ☐ wedding

 To practise vocabulary from this chapter, visit the Companion Website.

SPEAKING PRESENTATION TIPS

- PRACTISE YOUR PRESENTATION and time yourself. You should speak for about two minutes (or for a length determined by your teacher).

- USE CUE CARDS. DO NOT READ! Put about fifteen words on your cue cards.

- BRING VISUAL SUPPORT, such as a drawing, photograph, advertisement, or object. You can even prepare PowerPoint slides.

- CLASSMATES WILL ASK YOU SOME QUESTIONS about your presentation. You must also ask classmates about their presentations. Review how to form questions before the speaking test day.

Revising and Editing

The Revising and Editing sections at the end of each chapter help your students prepare for writing tests, including Benchmark and TESOL tests.

REVISE FOR AN INTRODUCTION AND EDIT FOR MODALS

A piece of writing should begin with an introduction. (To learn more about introductions, see Writing Workshop 2 on page 131.)

Read the short essay and follow these steps.

1 Underline and correct five verb or modal errors, not including the example.

2 Write a short introduction. It can consist of three or four sentences. End your introduction with a thesis statement. The thesis expresses the main focus of the essay.

Travel Tips

Introduction: _____

_____

_____

_____

_____

                                      bring   pack

First, carefully plan what you will ~~bringing~~. You should not ~~packing~~ too many clothes. You will want to buy souvenirs, so leave some extra space in your bag. Pack some medical supplies, such as bandages. Also, you

                  remove to

should ~~to~~ bring a very comfortable pair of shoes.

      Before you travel somewhere, learn about the country's requirements.

                     show

Canadians must ~~shows~~ a passport before they enter the United States.

                                          won't

Many countries also demand a visa. For example, China ~~wo'nt~~ let you enter the country unless you have a tourist visa.

      So remember to pack the necessities. Also learn about visa and passport

                                      have

requirements. If you prepare for your trip, you should ~~having~~ a great vacation.

Grammar TIP

Using *Will*

For the future tense, use the same form of the verb with every subject. Use *will* + the base form of the verb. The negative form of *will* is *will not* or *won't*.

           travel

He **will** ~~**travels**~~ with his wife.

He **won't buy** too many presents.

To learn more about the future tense, see Unit 6 in *Avenues 1: English Grammar*.

"It is never too late to have a happy childhood."

– AUTHOR UNKNOWN

CHAPTER 6

The Early Years

Our early years help shape the people that we will become. In this chapter, you will read about childhood in different nations.

Read each character trait out loud and ask students to raise their right hands if it is a female trait and their left hands if it is a male trait. Then discuss the results with the class.

Gender and Stereotypes

The **Innovative Association Test**[1] assumes that people make connections between familiar pairs of ideas. For example, if we hear the name "Caroline," we automatically associate it with a woman. Try the next test. Don't spend too much time thinking about your choice. Just put a check mark in either the female or male column.

FEMALE		MALE
☐	talks a lot	☐
☐	a fun parent	☐
☐	likes sports	☐
☐	cleans the house	☐
☐	supports the family financially	☐
☐	nags and complains	☐
☐	very emotional	☐
☐	has a good sense of direction	☐
☐	worries about appearance	☐
☐	aggressive	☐
☐	messy	☐
☐	likes to shop	☐

DISCUSSION

1. What are some common stereotypes about males and females? Compare the stereotypes with the reality.

2. How are stereotypes about gender harmful?

LISTENING PRACTICE

The listening segments are included in the Companion Website. You can assign the listening activities in class or give them as homework. Please note that there are additional questions online for the listening activity "Pink or Blue: Gender Stereotyping."

1. Pronounce Words

Practise pronouncing the following words. Pay attention to the pronunciation of the letters *h* and *th*. Read the following Pronunciation Tip.

Pronunciation **TIP**

Pronouncing *t* and *th*

When you pronounce *t*, the tip of your tongue touches the roof of your mouth. But when you pronounce *th*, the tip of your tongue should touch your top teeth.

Example   *bat*   *bath*

Repeat each pair of words after the speaker. Then you will hear a sentence. Underline the word that you hear in the sentence.

---

1 The Innovative Association Test (IAT) was developed by Anthony G. Greenwald, Mahzarin Banaji, and Brian Nosek.

1	tank	thank		5	three	tree		9	taught	thought
2	ear	hear		6	air	hair		10	bat	bath
3	math	mat		7	harm	arm				
4	hate	ate		8	tear	there				

2. Dictation

Practice your pronunciation by repeating each sentence after the speaker. Then write each sentence.

1	Who has three children?
2	I live with my family.
3	I thought that you taught math.
4	Our children are very young.
5	She threw something at him.
6	I don't know anyone here.
7	There are three things in the box.
8	The trees are beautiful.
9	He really wants different courses.
10	Thank you for thinking of me.

🔊 **LISTENING**

Pink or Blue: Gender Stereotyping

Listen to the interview with Mark Chen. Begin by listening to the first part of the interview and completing the vocabulary exercise. Then listen to the rest of the interview and answer the comprehension questions.

PRE-LISTENING VOCABULARY

- **slope:** angle or inclination of a surface
- **steep:** refers to the degree of the inclination

slope

steep slope

Additional questions appear in the Student Section of the Companion Website.

VOCABULARY

1 Listen to the first part of the interview. Fill in the blanks with the words that you hear.

Host: Mark Chen is a sociologist. Mark, what _____do_____ we know about gender and stereotyping? What _____does_____ the research say?

Chen: Well, parents expect different _____things_____ from sons than from daughters. In one study, the researchers put babies on a sloped table. Then they asked _____parents_____ to guess how steep the angle could be for their babies. You know, at what point would their babies be unable to crawl on the table? Parents were accurate with their _____sons_____, but they consistently underestimated their _____daughters_____. They just assumed that baby girls are not as agile as boys.

In fact, they were _____wrong_____. Female babies perform as well as males. So parents subconsciously limit their daughters and underestimate their _____physical_____ agility. Other studies show that parents treat baby boys more roughly than girls. Parents are more _____impatient_____ when boys cry.

COMPREHENSION

Answer the following questions.

2 A researcher gave six-year-old children identical drinks in pink and blue cups. Predictably, most boys preferred the drink in the blue cup, and the girls chose the pink cup. In the group of twenty children, how many recognized that the drinks tasted the same?

a. zero   b. one   c. two   d. three

3 What are the names of Chen's children?

Son: _____Nicolas_____   Daughter: _____Kim_____

4 Write the characteristics that show the main differences between boys' and girls' toys.

Typical "female" toys	Typical "male" toys
Types of toys:	Types of toys:
Fashion dolls such as Barbies	Workshops, toolboxes
Baking toys	Video games
Baby dolls	Cars
	Superhero action figures
What toys teach girls to do:	What toys teach boys to do:
Raise children and care for the family	Design and build houses
Cook	Care about cars
Worry about fashion and appearance	Work in computer industries
	Be heroes

5 What can parents do to avoid gender-stereotyping their children?

They can buy gender-neutral toys such as modelling clay and sports equipment. They can let children explore and take risks.

Because students must be able to ask and answer questions during their oral presentations, this book provides them with plenty of opportunities to practise question formation.

Childhood and Gender

Work with a partner. First, fill in the missing auxiliary. Then ask your partner the questions. Write his or her answers on the lines provided.

Partner's name: _____

The Past

1 What toys _____ did _____ you play with during your childhood?

Answer (list five items): _____

_____

_____

2 During your childhood, what _____ were _____ the most popular toys for boys?

Answer (list five items): _____

_____

_____

3 During your childhood, what _____ were _____ the most popular toys for girls?

Answer (list five items): _____

_____

_____

The Present

4 Who _____ are _____ current role models for young girls?

Answer: _____

5 Who _____ are _____ current role models for young boys?

Answer: _____

6 Who _____ do _____ you admire these days? List three people.

Answer: _____ _____ _____

WRITING

In a paragraph of about 100 words, write about your partner's answers to the questions.

Prepare for your reading tests by visiting the Companion Website. Click on "Reading Strategies" to find a variety of practice exercises.

Students can visit the Companion Website to practise reading strategies. Exercises are structured to help students do better in their reading tests, including Benchmark and TESOL tests.

Finding the Message

When you look for the main idea, you ask what the text is about. When you look for the message, you ask **why** the author wrote the essay. Often, writers explain a lesson that they learned. When you read, consider the message.

Sometimes the meaning of a reading is not immediately clear. You must search for the author's message by "reading between the lines." In other words, look for clues in the text, and use logic to make a guess about the author's meaning.

READING 6.1

Gerard Jones is an award-winning author and comic book writer. In this essay, he discusses the importance of childhood heroes. As you read, consider what the writer's message could be. What point is he trying to make?

GRAMMAR LINK

When you come to parentheses, underline the appropriate word. You can listen to this essay on the Companion Website and check your answers.

Killing Monsters

BY GERARD JONES

1 My first (memory / remember) is of tearing the monster's arm off. I crossed the sea, and then pretended to sleep until the monster entered quietly. When it came near me, I seized its massive arm. We battled until, in desperation, it pulled away, bleeding and screaming, and mortally wounded. That was quite a feat for a five-year-old.

2 My mother did not have a lot of high culture during her childhood, so she made sure (than / that) I was more fortunate. She put prints from the Metropolitan Museum on all the walls. She (taught / learned) me about art. She read classic literature to me at bedtime. Most of it rolled off me. The only one I remembered was Beowulf because he was a barbarian monster-slayer of a hero.

3 He was a terrible role model. He didn't do (none / any) of the things we want our children's heroes to teach. He didn't discuss solutions with the group. He didn't think first of the safety of others. He didn't try to catch the monster without harming it. Instead, he bragged and he killed. Yet, it was Beowulf I wanted to be. I made my mom read it to me over and over, and I caught her when she tried to skip the most gruesome parts. Running naked from the bath across the polyester carpet, I roared, "I'll fight to the death!"

4 I was (no / any) warrior in real life. I was a mama's boy. I liked kids who were not too wild. The prospect of kindergarten terrified me. But at home, in my own world, I could tear a pillow off the bed with a "rrrrrrarrr!" and see the monster running away in terror.

5 "You were an adorable barbarian," my mom said. Then she added, "But I wanted you to be cultured."

6 As it turned out, I did grow up fairly civilized. I was cooperative and conscientious. But I carried monster-slaying heroes inside me the whole time. Beowulf gave way to King Kong, then Batman, then James Bond.

7 In my thirties, I wrote a book, *The Comic Book Heroes*. That book excited comic book editors, and they invited me to try writing superhero stories. I did, and I was good at it. Soon I wrote for heroes like Batman, Spider-Man, and the Hulk. (Than / Then) I created new heroes.

8 As a superhero writer, I consciously resisted the violence of cheap entertainment. I minimized fight scenes and stressed intellectual content. My comic books earned citations from parent councils. But then, at a comics convention in Chicago, I had a conversation that turned my relationship with action heroes in a whole new direction.

9 The line of autograph seekers, mostly teenage boys, moved through. Then I saw

wounded: hurt or damaged

rolled off: didn't interest

Beowulf: hero from a classic epic poem

bragged: told everyone how great he was

gruesome: terrifying and disgusting

(her / hers). She looked about thirteen, with glasses, and she seemed shy. "Can I help you?" I asked.

10 She said her name was Sharon, and she lived in a small Wisconsin town. Then she said, "I just want to tell you that *Freex* is, in my opinion, the best comic book ever."

runaways: children who leave home and live in the streets
struggles: challenges

11 *Freex* is about teenage runaways. They (<u>live</u> / leave) in the streets. They are cut off from the world by their deforming superpowers, and they form a street gang for mutual protection. I cared about teenage runaways, and I wanted to represent their struggles in super-heroic form. I was excited about trying to mix natural teen dialogue with ferocious battles on the city streets. But my scripts just wouldn't work. I could not get the character scenes to flow smoothly into the fights. The readers seemed (agree / <u>to agree</u>) with me: sales were dropping. Not one fan had mentioned it at the convention. But then Sharon said it was the best comic ever.

12 I asked her why, and as she talked, her shyness dissolved. She loved the characters' personalities. She preferred Lewis, the charismatic leader. I said, "It sounds like the character development scenes must be your favourites."

13 "No!" she said, animated. "It's the fights!"

14 "The fights?" I asked.

15 Sharon responded quickly. "That's when you see their passion. And their passion (very / <u>really</u>) makes them powerful!"

16 I asked her what she felt in those scenes. "Well," she said awkwardly. "I am them when I am reading about them. So ... I feel powerful."

17 Sharon made me take a hard look at my own biases. I used fight scenes as a necessary evil to make kids read the more valuable contents of my stories. But now I wondered. The truly transformative element of the story was the violence itself. The violence helped a timid adolescent girl discover a feeling of personal power.

(753 words)

Source: Jones, Gerard. *Killing Monsters: Why Children Need Fantasy, Superheroes, and Make Believe*. New York: Perseus, 2002. Print.

Students can read the essay in class or as homework. There are additional questions in the Student Section of the Companion Website. You can verify if students have read the essay by checking their scores with the grade tracker.

COMPREHENSION

Answer the following questions.

1 When Jones was a little boy, why did he love Beowulf?

Beowulf fought and killed monsters.

2 Jones writes comic books about which superheroes?

Batman, Spiderman, The Hulk, Freex

3 Who is Sharon?

She is a young girl who liked Jones' comic book *Freex*.

4 What is *Freex* about?   Teenage runaways

5 At the convention, how many fans said that they love *Freex*?

a. one

b. ten

c. all of the fans

6 What does Sharon love the most about *Freex*?

a. The fights

b. The development of the characters

c. The costumes of the superheroes

Are the following sentences true or false? Circle T for "true" or F for "false."

7 When Jones was a child, he was exposed to art and literature. **(T)** F

8 Jones was scared to go to kindergarten. **(T)** F

9 *Freex* was Jones' most successful comic book. T **(F)**

10 What is the writer's message? What did Jones learn?

He learned that violence can be an important part of a comic book story.

WRITE DEFINITIONS

11 Identify five difficult words from the text. Write a definition for each word.

1. _____
2. _____
3. _____
4. _____
5. _____

WRITE QUESTIONS

12 Imagine that you will meet this author. Write five questions that you will ask Gerard Jones.

1. _____
2. _____
3. _____
4. _____
5. _____

Grammar TIP

Questions with *How*

Use *how* to create a variety of questions.

Question words	Refer to	
How old	age	**How old** are you?
How far	distance	**How far** is your city from here?
How long	length of time	**How long** did your book tour last?
How often	frequency	**How often** do you read?
How much/many	quantity	**How much** does the book cost?
		How many books did you sell?

For more information about question forms, see Unit 4 in *Avenues 1: English Grammar.*

 **SPEAKING**

Role Model

Think about someone who inspires you. Choose someone you know. Then compose ten questions that you would like to ask that person. Use past, present, and future tense verbs in your questions.

Interview your role model. In a two-minute presentation, give information about that person. Remember to prepare cue cards, and practise before your presentation.

Mawlid Abdoul-Aziz was born and raised in Somalia. In the next interview, he describes his childhood in Africa.

My Childhood in Somalia

INTERVIEW WITH MAWLID ABDOUL-AZIZ

1 **Where are you from?**

2 I'm from Hargeisa, which is a very conservative city in Somalia. In my culture, it is important to respect parents, teachers, and elders. Each parent, relative, neighbour, and friend has a very distinctive role to play in a child's life. Parents do not worry so much about the whereabouts of their children because a social network is available for parenting and guidance. Many people in the village watch the children. Regarding discipline, the male relatives punish boys. Friends and neighbours are considered as an extension of the family, so they can also punish boys. The situation for girls is the same; they are under the control of the female side of the family and the females in the village.

blessings: formal approval; benediction

slices: thin flat pieces

3 **How do parents and teachers discipline children in your village?**

4 They often spank or hit the children. Physical punishment is tolerated by the society, and it is not considered abuse. For instance, between the ages of four to six, I went to a Nadrasa, or religious school, and the teachers were very strict. They sometimes hit students with a bamboo cane. When I went to the public school, there was also physical punishment, but the teachers were nicer. On the coast of Somalia, discipline is less strict, which is possibly because they are exposed to other cultures.

5 What Somalis have in common is that parents and elders are always right and children cannot contradict them. Our parents' "blessings" are highly regarded. Blessings are something that we have to work for. Our daily actions will earn us blessings. In fact, getting the blessings of parents and elders is considered the key to a successful life. For example, a very successful businessman will say that he has everything he worked for because of his parents' blessings. In my generation, if a child showed disrespect to his parents, he could lose everything, and nobody would want to associate with him.

6 **What did you play with during your childhood?**

7 We made toys with scraps of junk. For example, we made cars and trucks with tin cans. We cut a soup can into slices to make wheels. We made the body of the car with larger cans. A mechanic told us where to place the brakes, so we would even have suspensions and brakes on the toy cars.

8 **When did the wars in Somalia occur? How did the war affect you?**

9 Between 1976 and 1982, Somalia was at war with Ethiopia, and then there was a civil war in Somalia after that. A lot of my childhood was affected by war. Planes bombarded our village. It was frightening, but it became a way of life. It is amazing what you can get used to.

10 Officially the government said they would only send adults to fight the war, but it wasn't true. Soldiers went to the markets and captured kids and took them to training camps. Everyone old enough to carry a gun was put in the army. A lot of kids had a "one-way ticket" to the front line. The soldiers came and kidnapped children.

11 I was always quite small, so I didn't look old, and I never got captured. I had to be very careful, though, whenever I saw people from the army. My younger brother was tall, so my parents wouldn't let him out of the house. My parents were worried that he would be taken. Luckily, he was never captured by the soldiers. When I was twelve years old, a lot of children from my neighbourhood were taken. Some friends just disappeared, and we never saw them again. Others came back with mental health problems. They didn't recognize me. They were traumatized by war, and some committed suicide. When I see Canadian children play video games about wars, it frustrates me. They do not realize what a terrible thing war is.

12 **Why did you eventually leave Somalia?**

13 To escape the war, I had to leave the country. When I was fourteen, I went to Ethiopia by myself. Luckily, I met a very nice lady who helped me get a UN scholarship. Emotionally, it was hard because I needed my parents and family, but I had a good understanding of my situation. I became independent very early. I learned to listen to my instincts about people. I also learned to be "street-smart." I learned to survive with very little, and I would not panic in a hostile environment. It gave me some self-confidence at a young age.

street-smart: intuitive about how people behave; able to survive in the streets

14 **How did you support yourself when you left Somalia?**

15 I learned to support myself in Ethiopia. The government gave me a small amount of money because I was a UN refugee, but I also did what people do in those situations. I went to a French school, and many of my classmates had rich parents. They sometimes wanted to buy horses, so I was the middleman who would find them a horse. I would travel to the countryside—where Europeans weren't allowed to go—and buy young horses. I sold them for a profit. I could earn enough to survive for six months. I could earn ten times what I paid for the horse.

(860 words)

Students can read the essay in class or as homework. There are additional questions in the Student Section of the Companion Website. You can verify if students have read the essay by checking their scores with the grade tracker.

VOCABULARY AND COMPREHENSION

1 Match the following words with their definitions. The paragraph numbers are in parentheses. Write the letters of the correct definitions in the spaces provided.

Terms		**Definitions**
1. strict (4)	e	a. used force to take children
2. elder (5)	b	b. anybody who is older than you
3. tin can (7)	d	c. battleground during a war
4. front line (10)	c	d. metal container that preserves food
5. kidnapped (10)	a	e. severe; firm

2 What is distinctive about the parenting style in Somalia?

Other family members and neighbours play a role in a child's life.

Parents don't worry about where their children are.

3 Briefly describe these two aspects of Mawlid's childhood.

Play: He made his own toys out of scrap material.

Discipline: Physical discipline was accepted in his culture. Parents, relatives, and neighbours all helped to discipline the children.

4 Why was Mawlid polite to his parents? _Somalis expect children to obey their elders._
Parents' blessings are very important.

5 Why did Mawlid's brother hide during the war? _His parents were worried that_
soldiers would take him to the front line.

6 How did Mawlid survive in Ethiopia? _He got some money from the government,_
and he bought and sold horses.

7 In Mawlid's neighbourhood, many children were captured and forced to fight. How were they different when they returned home?
Some never came back. Others had mental health problems.

8 What is Mawlid's opinion of violent video games?
He hates them.

DISCUSSION

1 What challenges did Mawlid face during his childhood?

2 Mawlid says, "When I see Canadian children play video games about wars, it frustrates me. They do not realize what a terrible thing war is." Should companies create violent video games? Why or why not?

Vocabulary
BOOST

Family Terms

Do not confuse these family-related terms:

Your **stepmother** is your father's wife. (She is not biologically linked to you.)

Your **mother-in-law** is your husband's or your wife's mother.

*My father remarried, and my new **stepmother** is very nice.*

*My wife's father died, and now my **mother-in-law** lives with us.*

PRACTICE

Practise using more family terms. Write the letters of the correct definitions in the spaces provided.

Terms

1. twins _____c_____

2. only child _____f_____

3. siblings _____e_____

4. spouse _____a_____

5. adopted child _____b_____

6. blended family _____d_____

Definitions

a. marital partner (The male is a *husband*; the female is a *wife*.)

b. child who is legally raised by those who are not the biological parents

c. two children born on the same date to the same mother

d. family created by joining two divorced spouses and their children

e. brothers and sisters

f. child with no brothers or sisters

SPEAKING

Watch an excerpt from the documentary *Hyper Parents and Coddled Kids*. You can also read about birth order and its impact on children.

Answers will vary.

If you assign the "birth order" writing topic, ask students to review Unit 10 in *Avenues 1: English Grammar*. The essay requires the use of comparative and superlative forms.

Birth Order

According to some researchers, birth order influences a person's personality. With your partner, assign each characteristic to the appropriate rank in a family. If any terms are unfamiliar, you can use your dictionary.

| perfectionist | high achiever | risk taker | jealous |
| spoiled | flexible | selfish | responsible |

Oldest child	Middle child	Youngest child
_____	_____	_____
_____	_____	_____
_____	_____	_____

WRITING

In an essay of about 250 words, write about birth order. First, explain your rank in the family. Are you the youngest, oldest, or middle child? Are you an only child? Do you have step-siblings? Describe your family.

In your second paragraph, explain the advantages and disadvantages of your birth rank by comparing yourself to someone else in our family. If you are an only child, compare yourself to someone who has brothers and sisters.

In your conclusion, write about your future plans. What size family do you want? Will you have many children? Why or why not?

READING 6.3

Jan Wong was *The Globe and Mail*'s first female correspondent in China. In this excerpt from her memoir, *Red China Blues*, Wong discusses the "Little Emperors" of China.

China's Little Emperors

BY JAN WONG

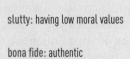

slutty: having low moral values

bona fide: authentic

1 When I first realized I was pregnant, Beijing seemed the perfect place to have a baby. After all, with a population of 1.2 billion, Chinese obstetricians must be pretty experienced. I was *The Globe and Mail*'s first female correspondent in China and thus the first to get pregnant on the job. I decided I could write some stories about childbirth and get an inkling of what I might be getting into.

2 I soon learned that Chinese hospitals treat you according to your status, or perceived status. Would they be brusque with me because they assumed I was a "passport girl"? (Although I am Canadian born and bred, many Chinese assumed that because my husband was white, I had to be a **slutty** local who had married a foreigner for his passport.) Or would they realize I was a **bona fide** foreigner and push me into having a Caesarean? More than one Chinese doctor told me that they prefer giving foreign women Caesareans to better control the birth. Having a foreigner die in childbirth would be an international embarrassment.

crawl: move on the ground using hands and knees

nanny: someone who is paid to take care of another person's children

guilt-free: having no culpability or remorse

tailor: person who makes clothing

ecstatic: thrilled; extremely happy

bristled: became annoyed

doted on: focused on and loved excessively

pulled a knife on: used a knife to intimidate

pampered onlies: spoiled, indulged children who have no brothers or sisters

3 While Chinese are renowned for loving children, having my own, first Ben in 1990, and then Sam in 1993, gave me a new perspective on child rearing. I discovered that most Chinese don't let babies crawl. An infant is always either in someone's arms or strapped to the mother's back. That makes sense because many peasants have dirt floors and most city dwellers have plain cement. Luckily, Ben went straight from sitting to walking, so I never had to argue with my nanny, Nanny Ma, about whether crawling could be permitted.

4 As a working mother in China, I felt remarkably guilt-free. In a society where all women have jobs, I was nothing special. In fact, the Chinese were pleasantly surprised that I kept my children with me at all. When the *Chinese Women's Journal*, a mass-circulation newspaper, profiled me, one of the first things it mentioned was the remarkable fact that I would not send my children back to Canada for someone else to raise.

5 Despite all the criticism of China's one-child restriction, it turns out that many parents can't, or won't, care for their own children. Chinese child-care experts estimate that between 5 and 10 percent of urban couples farm their one-and-only child off to relatives, sometimes in distant cities. My talented and very prosperous tailor, Huang Jianxing, was ecstatic when his wife had a baby boy in 1991. But six months later, they left their son to be raised by Huang's mother in Suzhou, one thousand kilometres south of Beijing. When I asked him why, he bristled. "I send my parents money all the time," he said.

6 In the one-child society, I began to feel self-conscious—even slightly guilty—whenever I walked down the street pushing Sam in the stroller, with Ben toddling along beside. "Look, she has two children," people would whisper, nudging one another. "Two sons!"

7 I started to wonder about the long-term repercussions of China's one-child policy. What will happen to a country where millions of children are growing up with no siblings, doted on by parents and grandparents? I saw six-year-olds still spoon-fed, and ten-year-olds who couldn't dress themselves. In a Beijing department store my sister Gigi, who was visiting me from Montreal, witnessed a three-year-old throwing a temper tantrum. "The parents and the grandparents were all crowding around, trying to get him to stop crying. They kept offering him toys, and he kept screaming louder. Finally, the father pulled out a pack of cigarettes and gave him one."

8 Some Chinese parents end up regretting their indulgence. When her son was young, Nanny Ma always saved him the freshest fruit. As a teenager, he still took the best for himself and said, in all seriousness, "But, Mom, you like bruised fruit." As he was growing up, she never let anyone, not even her husband, reprimand him. Once, when he was sixteen and addicted to video games, she wanted him to eat some juicy grapes, but she didn't want to interrupt him or get his fingers sticky. So she peeled one and put it into his mouth. Then another, and another. He glared at her. "Not so fast," he snapped. "Can't you see, I have to spit out the seeds?" A few years later, he pulled a knife on his mother when she objected to his girlfriend staying overnight.

9 Many people think that a country populated with Little Emperors is headed for disaster. I disagree. For generations, Chinese society has emphasized the family, the clan, the collective over the individual. Now, pampered onlies are growing up to be self-centred, strong-willed, knife-wielding individualists like, well, Americans. Where the Mao Generation failed, the Me Generation just might succeed. As one friend remarked to me, "It's China's salvation. If you have a population of Little Emperors, you can't have little slaves. Everyone will want to tell everyone else what to do. You'll have democracy."

(824 words)

Source: Wong, Jan. *Red China Blues*. Toronto: Doubleday, 1997. Print.

On the Companion Website, there are additional questions for "China's Little Emperors." You can assign the questions as a practice test or a formal reading test. Check students' scores with the grade tracker.

VOCABULARY AND COMPREHENSION

1 In China, most people have

a. three children   b. twins   c.) an only child

2 Find a word in paragraph 2 that means "a person from another country."

Foreigner

3 According to Wong, why don't Chinese babies crawl? (See paragraph 3.)

Many people have dirt or cement floors.

4 Why did people look at Wong when she walked on the streets? (See paragraph 6.)

a. They were mad at her because she was foreign.

b.) They were jealous that she had two sons.

c. They loved her beautiful clothing.

5 Describe Nanny Ma's son. What type of person is he?

He is very selfish. He does not respect his mother.

6 Wong calls China's children "Little Emperors." Give examples from the essay to show that some children are spoiled. (Their parents do not discipline them.)

A little boy cries until he gets a cigarette. Nanny Ma's son expects the best food. The author

describes six-year-olds who were spoon fed, and ten-year-olds who couldn't dress themselves.

7 What is the main idea of the essay?

a. China has a one-child policy.

b.) China's one-child policy is leading to a generation of spoiled only children, which may help the country achieve democracy.

c. People in China are only supposed to have one child, but Jan Wong has two children.

DISCUSSION

1 Wong wrote this essay in 1997. She predicted that a nation of only children will demand democracy. But China still has no democracy. Why?

2 What mistakes do some parents in China make?

3 Wong says that children in China are very spoiled. Are children in your country also spoiled? Give examples.

📺 WATCHING

This video has two sections. The first part covers a family's adoption of a child from Sudan and looks at celebrity adoptions. The second part covers a single mother's adoption of a child from Kazakhstan. Students can watch one or both parts of the video on the Companion Website. There are comprehensive questions for Parts 1 and 2 on the Companion Website.

Adoption

Adopting a baby from another country can be a joyful experience or a frustrating ordeal. Watch videos about adoptions and answer the following questions.

PRE-WATCHING DISCUSSION

Discuss the following questions with a partner or with the class.

1 Why do many people go to other countries to adopt children?

2 What are some of the positive and negative points of an international adoption?

3 In 2010, an American family returned an adopted child to Russia. What is your opinion about adoptive parents who change their minds?

Madonna with her adopted child

COMPREHENSION

As you watch the video, take notes. Summarize what happened. Write a paragraph about each part of the video. Include the following information.

PART 1: ADOPTION IN SUDAN AND CELEBRITY ADOPTIONS

· Why did Glen Pearson and Jane Roy go to Africa? *aid workers*
· What happened to Abouk's birth mother? *murder*
· What did Pearson and Roy discover when they returned to Africa? *twin sister older brother*
· Where does the family live? *London Ont.*
· In which country did Madonna adopt a child? *Malawi*
· Why was Madonna's adoption of her son controversial? *because his father is alive and wants to take/look after his son*

PART 2: ADOPTION IN KAZAKHSTAN

· What is Lindsey Drummond's marital status? *Single*
· What problems did Lindsey have when she tried to adopt in Canada?
· Why does Lindsey Drummond decide to adopt from Kazakhstan? *accessing Skype*
· What problems did she have in Kazakhstan? *Age/sick kids conflict disabilities legal issues arm miss*
· How much did she spend on the adoption? *42,000   31,000*

DISCUSSION

1 Why do Canadians go to so much trouble to adopt in foreign countries?

2 Madonna's child has a living parent. Some aid organizations believe that Madonna should help the father financially to raise his own child. What is your opinion? Should people be permitted to adopt poor children who have living parents?

Judge paperwork 6-8 / 10 weeks 2 months

Manitoba #1 married couple open cross prov adopt *Cash* *money not bent crisp dollars*

You can ask students to write their summaries in pairs. Another option is to ask students to write about one part and then share information with a partner.

no healthy children

Take Action!

Most of these topics can be either writing or speaking prompts. Additional writing and speaking topics appear in the Teacher Section of the Companion Website.

WRITING TOPICS

Write a 250-word essay on one of the following topics. For more information about how to structure an essay, see Writing Workshop 2 on page 131.

1 **Violence and the Media**

In "My Childhood in Somalia," Mawlid says, "When I see Canadian children play video games about wars, it frustrates me. They do not realize what a terrible thing war is." But in "Killing Monsters," Gerard Jones argues that violence in children's stories serves a useful purpose. Write about violence in video games and films.

· In a short introduction, explain why people like violent games and movies.

· Then, discuss your childhood. Did you play violent video games? Did you enjoy violent movies? Why or why not?

· In your third paragraph, express your opinion about violent games and movies. Should movies have less violence? Why or why not?

· In your conclusion, explain what you will do with your children. Will you permit them to play with violent games or watch violent movies?

2 Childhood and Culture

Read either "My Childhood in Somalia" (page 96) or "China's Little Emperors" (page 99). Compare your childhood to that of children in Somalia or China.

- Describe Mawlid's childhood, or describe children's lives in China.
- In the second paragraph, describe your own childhood. Did your parents spoil you? What were the good and bad points about your childhood?
- Then, make a comparison between the lives of children in this country and the lives of children in either Somalia or China. Which children have better lives? Which children have more difficult lives? Explain why.

3 Adoptions

Watch the Adoption video. Then write an essay about adoptions. Include the following information.

- Describe two of the adoptions. Choose from the adoption in Sudan, Madonna's adoption in Malawi, and the adoption in Kazakhstan.
- Then give your opinion on one or more of the following questions. Should Canadians adopt children from other countries? Was Madonna's adoption unethical because the boy's father was still alive? Should people adopt older children from Canada? Why do people prefer to adopt babies?

SPEAKING TOPICS

Prepare a presentation on one of the following topics.

1 Heroes

Discuss people who influenced you in the past and those who influence you today.

- In a short introduction, explain why people have heroes.
- Discuss your heroes when you were a child. Who did you admire? You can write about real people or about fictional heroes such as Superman.
- Then describe one or more people who influence you today. Who do you admire? Explain why.

2 Valuable Objects

Discuss items that are important to you.

- Present a very important object, toy, game, or technological item that you loved when you were a child. Who gave it to you? Did it have a useful purpose? Bring the object to class and describe it to your classmates.
- Then talk about an object that is important to you today. It can be anything that you own and value.
- Discuss the future. Explain what possession will be the most important to you. Think of something you currently own that will keep its value.

SPEAKING PRESENTATION TIPS

- PRACTISE YOUR PRESENTATION and time yourself. You should speak for about two minutes.
- USE CUE CARDS. DO NOT READ! Put about fifteen words on your cue cards.
- BRING VISUAL SUPPORT. You can bring a picture, photograph, video, PowerPoint slides, or an object.
- CLASSMATES WILL ASK YOU QUESTIONS about your presentation. You must also ask classmates about their presentations.

VOCABULARY REVIEW

Identify any words that you do not understand and learn their meanings.

- ☐ blended family
- ☐ childhood
- ☐ elders
- ☐ only child
- ☐ punish
- ☐ raise (a child)
- ☐ role model
- ☐ spoiled
- ☐ spouse
- ☐ stepbrother
- ☐ strict
- ☐ twin

If you assign Speaking Topic 2, you can do a preliminary game first. Ask students to write the name of a precious object on a small piece of paper. Then, in teams, students take turns either asking or answering questions. At each person's turn, he or she can only answer "yes" or "no." When someone guesses what the object is, that person collects the piece of paper. The person with the most papers wins the game. For instance, if a student writes "bracelet" others can ask "Did your boyfriend buy it for you?" "Is it made of metal?" etc. You can circulate and verify that students use correct question forms.

To practise vocabulary from this chapter, visit the Companion Website.

Revising and Editing

The Revising and Editing sections at the end of each chapter help your students prepare for writing tests, including Benchmark and TESOL tests. You can ask students to do the activities with a partner and share ideas.

EDIT SINGULAR AND PLURAL FORMS AND REVISE FOR A CONCLUSION

Practise editing an essay. Underline and correct ten errors to do with singular and plural forms, not including the example. Also write a concluding paragraph. It can be two or three sentences long. (For more information about writing a conclusion, see Writing Workshop 2 on page 135.)

             time
Our childhood should be a happy <u>times</u>. But childhood is difficult for

people   countries
<u>persons</u> in some <u>country</u>. They suffer a lot. In Canada, we are lucky because

children   lives
<u>childrens</u> have nice <u>lifes</u> compared to those in Somalia.

  First, when we read the story about Mawlid, we learned about the war in

Somalia. Soldiers sometimes captured children and made them fight. When

          year
Mawlid was a ten-<u>years</u>-old boy, he hid from soldiers. His brother could not

leave the house. Here in Canada, we do not have to worry about war. Our life

                      games
is very relaxed. During our childhood, we only think about our <u>game</u> and our

        worries
friends. We have no <u>worry</u>.

  Also, Mawlid had to leave his country by himself. He went to Ethiopia, and

he had to find a way to earn money. He could no longer live with his family.

              parents   children
In our country, we can stay with our <u>parent</u>. Most <u>childs</u> do not have to live

                     families
alone. Children have the financial and emotional support of their <u>familys</u>.

Conclusion: _____

_____

_____

_____

Grammar TIP

Plurals

Never add a plural ending to an adjective. Be careful because some nouns become adjectives when they modify another noun.

        noun   *adjective*
*The show costs 10 **dollars**.*   *We have three 10-**dollar** tickets.*

To learn more about plural forms, see Unit 5 in *Avenues 1: English Grammar.*

"Are we the Facebook generation? Are we the consumer generation or the green generation? The next generation will define who we are."

– JAYCE LYNDON (ARTIST)

CHAPTER 7

My Generation

What factors influence a generation? In this chapter, you will consider what makes your generation unique.

Generations

PART A

Look at the photos and imagine how people's lives were different in the past compared with today. Write a few ideas under each photo. How did people live at that time? Consider family life, gender roles, and technology in each era. Make some guesses.

1920	1950	2009

_____   _____   _____

_____   _____   _____

_____   _____   _____

_____   _____   _____

PART B

Compare the generations. Work with a partner and write six sentences about the photos. Your sentences should include the following words.

worse	larger	better
easier	harder	more expensive

1 _____

2 _____

3 _____

4 _____

5 _____

6 _____

Grammar TIP

Making Comparisons

Use comparative forms when you compare two people or things. Generally, when adjectives have one syllable, add *–er* to form the comparative.

> _Families are <u>smaller</u> today than they were in the past._

When adjectives have two or more syllables, add *more* to form the comparative.

> _People were **more** <u>independent</u> in the 1930s._

To learn more about comparative forms, see Unit 10 in *Avenues 1: English Grammar*.

READING STRATEGY

web+ Visit the Companion Website and click on "Reading Strategies" to find a variety of practice exercises.

Responding to a Text

After you read a text, reflect on what you have read. Then you can respond to the text with your own personal experiences and observations. Before you write a response, ask yourself the following questions:

· What are the main topics in the text?
· Do I agree or disagree with the writer?
· How does the text relate to my experiences?
· What observations can I make about my life?

READING 7.1

Are parents too overprotective these days? Read about some unusual parents. As you read, think about your own adolescence. Afterwards, you will respond to the reading.

A Lesson in Brave Parenting

BY BRUCE BARCOTT

1 Abby Sunderland is from Thousand Oaks, California. In 2010, the sixteen-year-old girl embarked on a non-stop sailing trip. Travelling alone, Abby hoped to become the youngest person to sail around the world. She travelled for 12,000 nautical miles. Then on June 10, she was in the Indian Ocean thousands of kilometres west of Australia when large **waves** broke the mast of her boat. She was able to activate emergency beacons, and authorities realized she was in trouble. Two days later, a French fishing boat rescued the teenager.

waves: surging rising water

2 What in heaven's name were her parents thinking? For a lot of people, that was the second thought that came to mind after hearing of Abby's rescue. The first thought, of course, was "Thank God she's alive."

3 Now that Abby is okay, the inevitable storm of criticism is raining down on her parents, Laurence and Marianne. They wished their daughter *bon voyage* when she cast off from Marina del Rey in January. They allowed a sixteen-year-old girl to sail alone around the world. Were they **insane**?

insane: crazy

4 Unusual, yes. But they are hardly "the worst parents in the world," as I heard them called recently. In fact, they may be the opposite. In a similar case, thirteen-year-old Jordan Romero climbed Mount Everest. Jordan's father, Paul Romero, and the Sunderlands are practising something rare these days: brave parenting.

5 I have an eleven-year-old and an eight-year-old. Raising kids today is like working on a construction site with an overzealous risk manager. Everywhere there are signs reminding parents that Safety Is Job One. Parents are told to cut up hot dogs and grapes to prevent choking, to place the kids into car seats, and to watch children vigilantly at the park. A certain amount of this is progress, of course. But in our obsession with safety, we are losing sight of the **upside** of risk, danger, and even injury. We can raise **bold** children who are prepared for adventure and eager to embrace the unfamiliar.

upside: good points; benefits
bold: courageous

6 The habitat of my own children is restricted. It contains entirely too many screens and couches. And this constraint is not unique to my family. Sandra Hofferth, a researcher at the University of Maryland, found that the amount of time kids spent outside doing things such as walking, hiking, fishing, and beach play declined by 50 percent between 1997 and 2003. Not long ago, up to half of the kids in this country walked or rode their bikes to school. Now fewer than one in five do. That inactivity has consequences. In the 1960s, fewer than 5 percent of American kids were obese. Now it's close to 20 percent. So seldom do kids wander in the woods that "nature deficit disorder" has become a common concern among parents of my generation.

7 The Sunderlands are not crazy. They are subversives. They are acting against a dominant culture that fills parents with fear. Parents blame themselves every time their child skins a knee.

8 To be clear, brave parenting is not synonymous with wise parenting. I have my own reservations about permitting a thirteen-year-old like Jordan Romero to climb Mount Everest. One veteran Everest climber told me, "I'm not sure a thirteen-year-old can be fully cognizant of the lethality of that environment." To me, the limit in these situations should be age sixteen.

9 While I question the wisdom of permitting a thirteen-year-old to go up a Himalayan peak, I cannot criticize the impulse behind it. I applaud it. Personally, I am not planning to climb Mount Everest with my eleven-year-old daughter. We won't even try Mount Rainier. That's not who she is. And if it were, she would still be too young. But the brave parenting of the Sunderlands and the Romeros forces me to reconsider the constraints I put on my kids. It helps me lead my son and daughter to the edge of the woods and tell them, "Go farther now, on your own."

(661 words)

Source: Barcott, Bruce. "A Lesson in Brave Parenting." *LA Times* 16 June 2010. Web.

COMPREHENSION

1 What did Abby Sunderland hope to do in 2010?

She wanted to become the youngest person to sail around the world.

2 When Jordan Romero tried to climb Mount Everest, how old was he?

Thirteen years old

3 What ideas are found in paragraph 5? Put a check mark (✓) beside three supporting points.

☑ The writer Bruce Barcott has two children.

☐ These days, children take too many risks and hurt themselves.

☑ Parents are too obsessed with the safety of their children.

☑ Risk and danger have positive points: children become more courageous and adventurous.

☐ Parents spend too much money on their children.

4 What is the writer's opinion of his own children's environment? See paragraph 6.

His children do not spend enough time outside. They spend too much time in front of the television or in front of a computer screen.

5 What is the writer's opinion of Abby Sunderland's parents?

a. They are crazy and dangerous parents.

(b.) They are courageous and subversive parents.

c. They are ordinary parents.

6 What is the main point of this text?

Parents should stop overprotecting their children, and they should allow their children to take risks.

_____

_____

WRITING

Respond to "Brave Parenting." Did you take risks when you were in high school? Did your parents set a lot of rules for you? In a 120-word paragraph, write about your adolescence.

Vocabulary BOOST

Let or Leave

Let means "to permit."

Leave means "to go away." It also means "to forget" or "to place in a specific location."

My parents **let** us borrow the car. We cannot **leave** the car on the street.

PRACTICE

Write _let_ or _leave_ in the blanks.

1 My parents are very easygoing. They _____let_____ me stay out late. I have no curfew. But they don't _____let_____ me drink and drive. If I drink, I have to _____leave_____ the car behind and take a taxi.

2 Sometimes my parents _____let_____ me have parties. Their only condition is that I clean up afterwards. If I _____leave_____ plates or glasses on the floor, my parents will be angry.

 Practise using _leave_, _let_, and other vocabulary from this chapter.

WATCHING

Students can answer additional questions for "Thrill Seekers" on the Companion Website. The questions can serve as a practice test or as a formal listening test.

Thrill Seekers

Why do some adolescents risk their lives by doing dangerous stunts? In the next video, you will learn about Type T personalities. Take notes as you watch the segment.

PRE-WATCHING VOCABULARY

Before you watch, review the meanings of the following vocabulary terms.

- **thrill:** excitement; stimulation
- **seeker:** searcher
- **excel:** be excellent in

COMPREHENSION

Answer the following questions.

1 What is skitching?

a. Holding onto a car while on a skateboard

b. Standing on top of a car

c. Riding a bike over large jumps

2 Chris and Kevin Sorichetti were really good at what extreme sport?

Freestyle Bmx Trick

3 How much money did the brothers accumulate in medical bills?

_500,000_

4 Shawn Nipper died at what age? _16_

5 How did Nipper die?

go fast _Car Surfer spreadeagle on hood_

6 At what age is the frontal lobe of a brain fully developed?

_25_

7 What is a Type T personality?

exploratory arousal in Nervous System fearlessness

8 According to Dr. Farley, what should parents do with their Type T children?

Channel them etc engage them

9 At the end of the video, you see Shaun White. What sport does he excel in?

snow board of parent involvem

10 How did Shaun White's parents respond to their son's Type T personality?

They encouraged it.

DISCUSSION

Do you know a Type T personality? Describe the person. What risky activities does he or she engage in?

🗨 **SPEAKING** # Parenting Rules

Discuss the following questions with a partner or in small groups.

1 Is it better for parents to be permissive or overprotective? Explain why.

2 From the perspective of a parent, discuss reasonable rules for adolescents. Consider the following issues. Think about youths between thirteen and fifteen years of age.

a. Curfew (an established time to be home at night)

b. Driving

c. Drugs and alcohol

d. Travel (without parents)

3 What should parents do when teenagers break the rules?

WRITING

In a 250-word essay, discuss rules for adolescents.

· First, explain which type of parent is better: a permissive parent or an overprotective one.

· Then describe your childhood and adolescence. What rules did your parents or guardians set? Were they permissive or overprotective? Describe a time when you broke a rule or made a bad decision. What happened?

· Finally, explain what rules you will set for your children. Also explain what type of parent you will be.

Using *Should*

When you give advice, you can use the modal auxiliary *should* + the base form of the verb. Avoid the following errors.

· Never add *–s* or *–ed* to the verb that follows *should*.

watch
A small child should not <s>watches</s> too much television.

· Never put *to* between *should* and the verb.

You should <s>to</s> discipline children with love.

To learn more about modal auxiliaries, see Unit 9 in *Avenues 1: English Grammar*.

Ruth Wade was born in 1934 in Medicine Hat, Alberta. She came of age in the 1940s and early 1950s. Her generation, sometimes called the "Silent Generation," had particular qualities. In the interview, Wade discusses various characteristics of her generation.

The Silent Generation

AN INTERVIEW WITH RUTH WADE

1 How did World War II[1] impact your childhood?

2 I was five years old when the war began. The war was far away but it affected us. I worried about people who went to fight. Our neighbour, Johnny, often talked to us kids and we really liked him. He was only nineteen years old when he died fighting overseas.

3 There was no television in those days, so we learned about the war during newsreels at the local cinema. We also listened to one radio show a day. I did not see a television until I was in my twenties.

4 During your youth, how did teenagers rebel?

5 Probably the riskiest thing we did was have drag races. On country roads, guys would race each other. A few bad accidents happened. Cars did not have seatbelts, so drag races were pretty risky.

6 Also, some youths tried to stand out and look different. Most young men had short hair, but some got Mohawks. They were considered pretty hip. Later, in the 1950s, when Elvis Presley was popular, guys had ducktails. They would let the hair grow long over

---

1 World War II occurred from 1939 to 1945.

the ears and keep it shorter on top. My brother had a ducktail and my father hated it. Dad often threatened to cut off the ducktail while my brother was sleeping.

7 In the 1940s, our parents wore hats when they went out shopping or whatever. My generation stopped wearing hats. Maybe the boys were too worried about their hair.

8 How was family life different during the 1950s?

9 Divorce was rare. Even when marriages were very violent or horrible, couples usually stayed together. Most people had at least four or five children. Families were united. On weekends, the whole family would go to dances or play card games, and the babies would sleep in the corner.

10 How were single mothers treated in those years?

11 It was terrible for girls who got pregnant. One girl I knew had a baby when she was fifteen. She was a really nice, quiet girl. After she had the baby, everybody shunned her. Nobody wanted to associate with her. They also treated her son badly just because he had no father. Sometimes, to avoid a scandal, the girl's parents would pretend that the baby was theirs.

12 Was abortion an option during those decades—the 1940s and 1950s?

13 In those days, abortion was illegal[2]. Of course, backstreet abortions happened, and sometimes the girls got sick or died. They used coat hangers, and conditions were unsanitary. There was another terrible thing that women did. Sometimes women ate a small amount of gopher poison to provoke an abortion. The poison would cause a miscarriage.

14 People today don't realize how difficult it was for girls in the past. Unwed mothers were called **tramps** and ostracized, so girls were really scared to get pregnant.

tramp: derogatory term meaning "promiscuous woman"

15 How were gender roles different?

16 Well, women worked in factories during the early 1940s because the men went off to war. However, there was a law that when the men came back at the end of the war, employers had to give the jobs to the veterans. At our local glass factory, the women were **fired** when the men returned. It was fair, I think, because those veterans needed their jobs.

fired: removed from their jobs

17 Girls usually didn't continue schooling, but my father was rare, and he encouraged me to go to university. I received a scholarship and did one year at university before I got married.

18 How old were you when you got married?

old maid: insulting term for an unmarried woman

I was nineteen. If a girl was twenty-five and single, people would call her an **old maid**. My marriage was controversial because my family was Protestant, and I married a Catholic. My father refused to come to my wedding. People were more religious, but they were also more intolerant.

19 I had four children, but I was very bored being a housewife. So, when my youngest child was in school, I took a job teaching. Some neighbours insulted my husband by saying things such as, "I guess you can't afford to support your wife." It was difficult for us because women were expected to stay home and take care of the family.

(711 words)

---

2 In Canada, 19th-century legislation outlawed abortion. Then, in 1988, Canada's Supreme Court ruled that the law was unconstitutional. Currently, there is no law against abortion.

COMPREHENSION

What are the main features of Ruth Wade's youth? Complete the chart with descriptions of various aspects of life for people of the silent generation.

Politics

War: World War II happened. Ruth worried about those who went to war.

·Laws: Abortion was illegal. People had dangerous illegal abortions.

Technology

There was no TV. People got information from the radio or newsreels.

Family Life

Women were expected to marry before age 25. Families were large. Divorce was rare. Couples stayed together even when there were problems.

Gender Roles

Women were supposed to stay at home. People were rude to Ruth's husband when she got a job as a teacher.

Religion

Religion was important. Ruth's father didn't come to her wedding because she married a Catholic

---

WRITING

Using a separate sheet of paper, follow these steps.

1. Identify five difficult words in the text. Write a definition for each word.

2. Write five more questions that you would like to ask Ruth.

3. In a paragraph of about 120 words, summarize the text "The Silent Generation." Mention at least five key features of this generation. Use your own words. Do not copy exact phrases from the text.

◀)) LISTENING PRACTICE

1. Identify Silent Letters

Repeat each pair of words after the speaker. Then circle the silent letter in each pair of words. (For rules about silent letters, and for other pronunciation tips, see Appendix 4 on page 144.)

EXAMPLE: *listen castle*   l   (t)

			SILENT LETTER				SILENT LETTER
1	know	knife	(k)	n	6	hour	honest	(h)	o
2	thumb	climb	m	(b)	7	walk	talk	(l)	k
3	design	sign	(g)	n	8	plumber	comb	m	(b)
4	should	could	(l)	d	9	often	listen	n	(t)
5	write	wrong	r	(w)	10	thought	light	(gh)	t

2. Identify Words

Listen to each sentence and underline the words that you hear. Listen carefully to word endings.

¹Kate Lund likes to take risks. She knows that she (should / <u>shouldn't</u>). ²However, she (can / <u>can't</u>) stop herself. She is a risk taker.

³Last (Tuesday / <u>Thursday</u>), Kate decided to try car surfing. ⁴The 19-(years / <u>year</u>)-old woman was with her boyfriend Matt. ⁵Kate decided to (<u>climb</u> / climbing / climbed) onto the roof of the car, and Matt drove. ⁶It (was / isn't / <u>wasn't</u>) a good idea. ⁷When Matt stopped at a stop (sing / <u>sign</u>), Kate fell off the roof. ⁸She hurt (his / <u>her</u>) back, but she survived. ⁹These days, she is lucky that she (<u>can</u> / can't) still walk.

¹⁰The police charged Matt with dangerous driving. He (can / <u>can't</u>) leave the province. ¹¹He (<u>can</u> / can't) speak with his friends. ¹²However, he (can / <u>can't</u>) drive a car. ¹³Matt (<u>could</u> / couldn't) lose his licence. ¹⁴Kate (should / <u>shouldn't</u>) car surf again! ¹⁵Hopefully, Kate and Matt (can't / will / <u>won't</u>) make the same mistakes in the future.

🔊 LISTENING

Generation Y: Coming of Age in the 1990s

Natalia MacDonald was born in 1982, and she came of age in the 1990s. Natalia discusses her generation.

COMPREHENSION

Are the following sentences true or false? Circle T for "true" or F for "false."

1. Natalia's generation did not have to fight for women's rights.   (T)   F

2. Generation Y is more politically active than the previous generation.   T   (F)

3. Natalia had a cellphone when she was a little girl.   T   (F)

4. Natalia first used the Internet when she was at the end of high school.   (T)   F

5. What were three problems or inconveniences with the early Internet?

It was very slow.

You couldn't talk on the phone at the same time as you used the Internet.

You had to use the same e-mail account as everyone in your family.

6. What was the most popular musical style for Generation Y?

a. punk   (b.) grunge   c. rap

7. What were some fashion trends in the 1990s? Choose four answers.

☐ black hats   ☑ ripped jeans

☑ Converse running shoes   ☐ white dresses

☑ ball chains   ☑ oversized flannel shirts

Kurt Cobain (Nirvana)

8 What world events shaped Natalia's generation? Name two events.

First Gulf War, death of Princess Diana, and 9/11

9 What is the main worry facing Generation Y?

a. war   b. the environment   c. unemployment

10 What did Natalia study at university?

Political science   Masters

In the Take Action! section, there are writing and speaking prompts. Students can compare their generation to Generation Y.

DISCUSSION

1 How is your generation different from Generation Y?

2 What is a good name for your generation?

 **READING 7.3**

Some groups of people have distinct fashion styles, musical interests, beliefs, and behaviours. Read about some of the most interesting subcultures.

Three Subcultures

BY A. BERRIDGE

"Three Subcultures" can be a team-reading activity. Read the introduction with the class, and then divide students into three groups. Each group reads one section and then explains what they have read to people in the other groups.

1 In the past one hundred years, many youths, searching for an identity outside college, family, or work, created lifestyle groups. These subcultures focus on music, fashion, politics, and occasionally a specific activity such as skateboarding or computer hacking. Subcultures can involve upper-class students (preppies), working-class youths (greasers), sensitive young men and women (emos), the garage band casual types (grunge), to name a few.

2 Certain subcultures are "countercultures." They are counter—or opposed to—the established culture of the era. Here are three of the most interesting subcultures of the last one hundred years. All three of these groups were originally marginalized. Early adherents were fired from jobs and kicked out of schools. Some families even disowned children who embraced these movements. Eventually, all three movements went mainstream and had long-lasting impacts on social life, fashion, and music.

PART A: FLAPPERS (1920s)

arose: began
booming: doing well

3 In the 1920s, the flapper movement **arose** during a period of prosperity. North American economies were **booming**. The car became affordable to the middle classes. Women received the right to vote in the US (1920) and in most Canadian provinces (1919). So life was good before the 1929 stock market crash.

4 Flappers were independent young women who broke conventions. They refused to wear the long heavy dresses and corsets of their mothers, and instead wore knee-length dresses. Since legs were considered highly sexual features of a woman's body, this public exposure of legs was scandalous. Also, women stopped padding their rears to look more shapely. Instead, they wrapped up their chests to look like boys. Flappers also broke social conventions by wearing rouge and lipstick. At the time, makeup was

associated with prostitutes, so parents were upset when their daughters applied cosmetics. Flappers also scandalized their parents by cutting their hair short.

5 Social life changed in that era. The predominant music was jazz, and black musicians such as Louis Armstrong were popular. Flappers smoked, danced alone to the Charleston, and drove motorcars. Most critically, relations between the genders changed. A girl could hold a man's hand without wearing gloves. Before the 1920s, girls did not spend time alone with a man unless he was interested in marriage. The new generation of females wanted more control over their social lives. For the first time, a female could date different males and still have the respect of her social group. Thus, the flapper culture had long-lasting impacts on social relations and was a precursor to the women's rights movement of the 1960s.

PART B: HIPPIES (1960s)

6 The original hippie movement started in the early 1960s. One of the instigating factors of the American hippie movement was the Vietnam War. From 1965 to 1973, the United States expanded its efforts to eradicate communism from Vietnam. According to the US Veteran's Administration, roughly nine million American soldiers fought in that war. About two million men were "drafted." They did not volunteer to fight; instead, their birthdates were randomly chosen, and they were ordered to fight. About 58,000 young American soldiers died during that war.

7 Many hippies were involved in political movements. Feeling frustrated with the loss of lives in Vietnam, they held mass demonstrations and asked for "peace and love." Canada became the recipient of over 100,000 draft dodgers—young men whose birthdays were called in the draft lottery, and who did not want to fight in Vietnam. Also, during the 1960s, the women's movement exploded, with women demanding equal pay for equal work. Martin Luther King guided the American civil rights movement. So the original hippie era saw massive changes in the rights of women and minorities.

The Beatles

8 The music most closely associated with the hippie era was psychedelic rock—by bands such as the Beatles, Jefferson Airplane, and Grateful Dead. Male hippies broke with convention by growing their hair long, which was radical in an era when most men had very short crew cuts. Female hippies stopped wearing makeup and let their long hair flow. Tie-dyed clothing and peace signs were popular.

9 Hippie culture spread through Canada, Mexico, Europe, and eventually went global. Even young Russians, during the height of the Cold War, grew out their hair and listened to the Beatles. The original hippie movement ended in the early 1970s, after musical icons Jimi Hendrix and Janis Joplin died from drug overdoses.

PART C: PUNKS (1976-1986)

10 In 1976, the punk movement exploded in both New York and London. In the US, the optimism of the "peace and love" years was over. In England, unemployment was widespread. Both countries saw the sudden emergence of a new youth movement that spread to other nations. Adherents were bored with the sentimental light rock of bands such as the Eagles. Critic Robert Christgau said, "It was also a subculture that scornfully rejected the political idealism and Californian flower-power silliness of the hippie myth."

lottery: In a large glass container, 366 blue capsules contained birthdates, and every date was assigned a number. When their numbers came up, all men between the ages of eighteen and twenty-six had to report for military service.

Cold War: From 1947 to 1991, there was military tension between the Western world and Communist nations.

widespread: common across a large area

scornfully: with derision or contempt
silliness: absurdity; superficiality

lack: absence

11 In the United Kingdom, punk rock was most clearly exemplified by the loud raw music of the Sex Pistols. Amateur musicians, they glorified their lack of musical skills, playing simple and aggressive tunes such as "Anarchy in the UK" and "No Future." Other early punk bands were The Clash and Siouxsie and the Banshees. Their songs spoke of unemployment, hopelessness, and anger at a corrupt society. Offering no solutions for society's problems, they advocated anarchy.

ripped: torn; broken

12 In 1976, a young punk did not need to have money. Original punk fashion was based on reusing and recycling everyday items. Punks wore large black work boots and old ripped jeans and T-shirts held together with safety pins. Punks wore safety pins in their pierced lips, ears, and eyebrows. Using felt pens and spray paint, punks created graffiti art on their clothing. Mohawk hairstyles, spiky hair, and vibrant hair colours helped punks stand out.

The Sex Pistols

high-end: expensive

13 Over time, the punk movement went mainstream. The fashions appeared in high-end stores, and punk music fragmented into different styles. Talented bands such as Green Day and Offspring became massively popular. These days, punk influences are found in fashion, art, and music.

(988 words)

Sources: Cooper, Ryan. "A Brief History of Punk." *The History of Punk Rock. About.com.* 2010. Web.
Rosenberg, Jennifer. "Flappers in the Roaring Twenties." *Twentieth Century History. About.com.* 2010. Web.
Rosmen, Jennifer. "The Hippy Counter-Culture." *Associated Content.* Yahoo Contributor Network. 2007. Web.

VOCABULARY AND COMPREHENSION

PART A: FLAPPERS (1920s)

1 Write the letters corresponding to the pictures in the spaces provided. The paragraph numbers are in parentheses.

1. Padded rear (4)   A

2. Knee-length dress (4)   C

3. Gloves (5)   B

A
B
C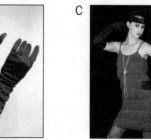

2 What was happening in society at the time of the flappers?

a. It was a time of economic prosperity.

b. It was a difficult time; people suffered economically.

3 How were flappers different from their mothers?

They had more freedom and could vote.

They liked jazz. They cut their hair short and wore knee-length dresses.

They could date men.

PART B: HIPPIES (1960s)

4 What was the "draft"?

People were forced to join the military. Hippies did not volunteer to become soldiers.

5 What did hippies protest about? List three things.

There was a war in Vietnam. People protested against the war. Hippies wanted women's rights and

minority rights.

6 Write the letters corresponding to the pictures in the spaces provided. The paragraph numbers are in parentheses.

1. Crew cut (8)   C

2. Peace sign (8)   B

3. Tie dye (8)   A

A    B    C

PART C: PUNKS (1976-1986)

7 What were early punk songs about?

Unemployment, hopelessness, and anger at a corrupt society

8 What does punk continue to influence?

Fashion, graffiti art, and music

9 Write the letters corresponding to the pictures in the spaces provided. The paragraph numbers are in parentheses.

1. Safety pin (12)   B

2. Work boots (12)   C

3. Spiky hair (12)   A

A    B    C

What are the main features of each subculture? List some characteristics in the spaces beside the various categories.

	Flappers	**Hippies**	**Punks**
Social Context	Prosperity; women got the right to vote	Vietnam war; protests for women's rights and civil rights	Unemployment; peace and love optimism was over
Clothing and Hair	Knee-length dresses with no corsets; short hair	Long hair on men; tie-dyed shirts and peace symbols	Ripped jeans and shirts held together with safety pins; spiky hair
Music	Jazz (Louis Armstrong)	Psychedelic rock (Beatles, Grateful Dead)	Punk (The Clash, Sex Pistols, Siouxsie and the Banshees)
Beliefs and Attitudes	Women could date; women could wear makeup and show their legs	Rights for women and minorities; end the war	Anger; anarchy; musical skills don't matter

Students can write about subcultures in the Take Action! section.

DISCUSSION

Think of some of today's subcultures. Describe the music they listen to, the clothing that they wear, and the beliefs that they hold.

... SPEAKING

As a speaking activity, you can ask team members to choose one of the categories in the chart and then present information about that topic. They should use examples from their lives and from the lives of people they know.

The Current Generation

Discuss the current generation. Fill in the chart with information.

Political and Social Issues (List five problems that concern your generation.)

_____

Technology

_____

Music

_____

Family Life

_____

Religion

The chart can become the basis for a writing test. You can ask students to write about key features of their own generation.

Take Action!

These topics can be used as individual or team writing or speaking tests. For additional topics, visit the Teacher Section of the Companion Website. Click on "Writing" or "Speaking" to find a list of topics.

These very structured writing topics work well in final writing tests.

Write about one of the following topics. For information about essay structure, see Writing Workshop 2 on page 131.

1 Subcultures

Write a paragraph or essay about a current subculture.

· Describe the music, fashions, and attitudes of that subculture.

· Provide specific examples of people who are in that subculture.

2 Thrill Seeking

Write about people who take extreme risks. Your essay should discuss the following points.

· In a short introduction, define a thrill seeker.

· Explain why movies such as *Jackass* are so popular. Why do some people take extreme risks, doing activities such as car surfing?

· Then describe your childhood. Were you a risk taker? Did you or your friends do dangerous activities? Why or why not? Include a story about something that you or your friend did.

· In your conclusion, explain what you will tell your children about risk taking.

3 Generations

Describe your generation and another generation. You can discuss the Silent Generation or Generation Y. You can also discuss flappers, hippies, and punks. Your essay should discuss the following points.

· In a short introduction, explain how generations change over time.

· Describe a past generation. If you choose a generation that was described in this chapter, do not use exact words or phrases from the text. Use your own words.

· Then describe your generation. What makes it unique? Use examples from your life and from the news. You can also use ideas from the "Current Generation" chart on page 119.

· In your conclusion, explain which generation will have a larger impact on history and the world.

4 Music

Every generation has its own musical forms. The Silent Generation listened to Big Band and Swing. The Baby Boomers listened to rock music such as the Beatles. What music is important to your generation? Write an essay that includes the following components.

· In a short introduction, explain why music is important. Why do all cultures have music?

· Discuss current music. Who do you listen to? Describe some singers who are popular today. Why do people like some singers or songs?

· Describe some important music from the past. You can describe music that you loved when you were a child. Give examples of specific singers, songwriters, or groups. What were the songs about?

· In your conclusion, predict which musicians will still be popular in the future. Who will people still listen to in fifty years?

Note: Always put *to* after *listen*. You listen **to** music.

SPEAKING TOPICS

Prepare a presentation about one of the following topics.

1 Life Lesson

Present an experience that changed your life. You can discuss something that happened to you or to someone you know. You can also discuss something that happened in the world. To get ideas, ask yourself the following questions: Did you ever hurt someone? Did you help someone? Did you make a very good or bad decision? Did someone you know make a life-changing mistake? Did an event in the news affect you?

· Begin by explaining what happened. Give details.

· Then explain how the event changed your life. How are you different today?

· In your conclusion, explain what you will teach your children.

2 A Problem in Society

Present a problem in society. Choose something that you know well.

Possible topics: body image, drug use, dropout rates, drinking and driving, smoking laws, gambling, environmental problems, your choice

· Begin with a personal story about the problem. Describe what happened to you, someone you know, or someone who is well-known. Give details.

· Then suggest a solution. What should people do?

· In your conclusion, explain what you will teach your children.

3 Public Service Announcement Video

Work with a partner or a team. Videotape a public service announcement. Your announcement should be about two minutes long. Convince viewers to be careful. Choose one of the following topics:

– Texting while driving

– Drinking and driving

– Drugs

– Car surfing

– Cheating in college courses

– Corruption in politics

– Internet or social networking addictions

– Your own topic

SPEAKING PRESENTATION TIPS

· PRACTISE YOUR PRESENTATION and time yourself. You should speak for about two minutes.

· USE CUE CARDS. Do not read! Put about fifteen words on your cue cards.

· BRING VISUAL SUPPORT. You can bring a picture, photograph, DVD, CD, video, PowerPoint slides, or an object.

· CLASSMATES WILL ASK YOU QUESTIONS about your presentation. You must also ask classmates about their presentations.

VOCABULARY REVIEW

Review key terms from this chapter. Highlight the words you do not understand and learn what they mean.

☐ bold

☐ curfew

☐ impact

☐ knee-length

☐ leave

☐ let

☐ misbehave

☐ overprotective

☐ pregnant

☐ ripped

☐ sail

☐ thrill seeker

 To practise vocabulary from this chapter, visit the Companion Website.

Revising and Editing

REVISE FOR SENTENCE VARIETY

A piece of writing should have some sentence variety. In the next essay, combine some of the sentences to form new sentences, using the following words.

and   so   but   because   when

EXAMPLE: He took risks. ~~He~~ tried car surfing. *, and*

I made a big mistake, *when* I was fifteen. I took the car, *, but* I didn't have my driver's licence. My parents were not home. ~~The~~ keys were on the table. *,and the* I asked my twin brother to come with me. We planned to drive around the block. ~~Then~~ we *, and then* would return home. I felt hungry, *, so* I drove to a fast-food restaurant. I saw my friends at the restaurant. ~~They~~ wanted me to drive them home. *, and they* I was scared, ~~We~~ got in the car and drove. My friends wanted me to drive faster. *, but we*
I agreed, *because* I did not want to disappoint my friends.

EDIT FOR MIXED ERRORS

Read the paragraph and correct ten errors. Look for errors in comparisons, plurals, verb tenses, and subject–verb agreement. Also look for one capitalization error.

We drove on the main boulevard, and the car went ~~more~~ faster than before. I didn't <u>knew</u> how to brake correctly. I lost control, and two <u>others</u> *know* *other* cars almost hit us. I parked on the side of the road, and I asked <u>ours</u> friends *our* to get out of the car. Then my brother and I <u>return</u> home. When we arrived, *returned* my parents <u>was</u> in the house. They looked furious. *were*

My father grounded me for three weeks. I <u>cannot</u> go out on weekends. *could not* After that, I did not <u>drove</u> for two years. I waited until <u>i</u> had a driver's licence. *drive* *I*

I wanted to be a ~~more~~ better driver before I used the car again.

This text is adapted from a short story written by Frank R. Stockton, an American writer and humorist, in 1882. The story describes a very strange kingdom and a very difficult choice.

The Lady, or the Tiger?

BY FRANK STOCKTON

Part 1

1 A long time ago, a barbaric king ruled with great authority. He had strange ideas, and because he was so powerful, he could act on any of his notions. He wanted his home and his nation to run smoothly.

2 In the kingdom, there was a public arena where the people watched exhibitions of valour. But even there, the king exerted his barbaric ideas. The king's arena was not intended to show gladiators fighting against large dangerous beasts. Its purpose was to develop the mental energies of the people. Crime was punished, or virtue rewarded, by impartial and incorruptible chance. When someone was accused of a very serious crime, that person's fate would be decided in the public area, and the public would watch the spectacle.

fate: destiny

3 When everyone assembled in the arena, the king gave the signal from high up on his throne for the accused to step into the amphitheatre. The accused faced two doors that looked exactly the same, and it was his duty to open one of the doors. Behind one door was a fierce and hungry tiger, which would immediately tear him to pieces as punishment for his crime. Then bells would ring and the spectators would walk home, feeling very sad that someone so young or so old had to die in that cruel way.

4 But if the accused opened the other door, a lovely young lady would come out. The king always chose a woman who matched the age and social status of the accused man. The man would marry the beautiful lady as a reward for his innocence. It didn't matter if the man was already married; the king would not allow that fact to interfere with his system of justice. Bells would ring and people would shout in joy as the man led his new bride to his home.

5 The king's method of administering justice, though barbaric, was obviously fair. The accused didn't know which door concealed the lion and which door concealed the beautiful lady. Heavy curtains ensured that the criminal could not hear any sound from behind the doors. The judgment was final as well as fair; the criminal would either be devoured or married depending on whether he was guilty or innocent.

slaughter: violent killing

6 In the kingdom, the trials in the arena were very popular. When people gathered on trial days, they did not know if they were going to witness a bloody slaughter or a fabulous wedding. The uncertainty entertained and pleased the masses. Even the more intelligent members of the community concluded that the practice was fair because the accused held his future in his own hands.

Additional comprehension questions appear on the Companion Website.

Answers will vary.

COMPREHENSION

1 What type of person was the king? Use three adjectives to describe him.

Cruel, authoritarian, barbaric, powerful

2 What determined a person's guilt?

a. The king's judgement b. Evidence c. Pure chance

3 Was polygamy possible in the kingdom? (Could a man have more than one wife?)

Yes ☑ No ☐

4 If the accused chose the door that concealed a lady, what happened?

He would be free, but he would have to marry the woman.

Part 2

7 The king had a daughter who was as passionate and imperious as her father. Naturally, the king adored his daughter and loved her above all humanity. One day, the daughter met a young man who was handsome and brave. But he was also poor and of a lower class than the princess. For many months, the couple met in secret. Then one day, the king found out about their meetings. The young man was immediately sent to prison and ordered to stand trial in the king's arena.

8 The whole kingdom was searched for the largest and most savage tigers. Competent judges also evaluated women from across the land and chose the most beautiful one. Of course, everybody knew that the young man was guilty of loving the king's daughter, but this did not stop the king. He wanted to go through with the trial and get rid of his daughter's **suitor** one way or the other.

suitor: lover; boyfriend

9 The day finally arrived, and everyone in the kingdom came to the arena. The king and his daughter sat in their places opposite the twin doors that looked so similar, yet held such different results for the accused. The people in the arena were quiet as the young man entered. The spectators admired the tall and handsome man and understood why the princess loved him. The accused turned to **bow** to the king, but he could not take his eyes off the lovely princess who sat next to her father.

bow: incline the head to show respect and submission

10 The princess was very interested in what would happen to the young man. She thought of nothing else from the moment she heard about the trial. Because she had so much power and influence, she managed to do what was almost impossible. Earlier that day, she discovered the secret. She knew which door concealed the tiger and which concealed the lady.

11 Not only did she know which door hid the lady, but she also knew who the chosen woman was. She was one of the most beautiful women ever selected for the arena, and the princess hated her. She had seen the woman and her lover exchange a few words. Maybe they were talking about something unimportant, but how was the princess to know? Another time, a few weeks earlier, the beautiful young woman made the mistake of raising her eyes to look at the young man, so the princess hated her intensely.

12 In the arena, the young man turned his frightened, pale face towards the princess. He immediately knew that she had figured out which door hid the tiger behind it. He had always hoped that she would find out. He looked at her anxiously, clearly asking, "Which door?"

13 The princess casually raised her hand and made a quick movement toward the right side. Only her lover saw her. Everyone else in the arena was watching him. He turned, and with rapid steps, he walked across the vast space. Then, without any hesitation, he went to the door on the right and opened it.

5 Why did the king disapprove of the princess's lover?

The young man was poor and from a lower class than the princess. He was not someone that the

king would choose for his daughter.

6 Where did the king sit in the arena?

Opposite the two doors

7 How did the princess feel about the lady behind the door?

The princess was jealous of the lady, and hated her.

8 How did the princess indicate the right door?

She moved her hand quickly to point to the door on the right side.

Part 3

14 The point of the story is: Did the tiger come out of the door on the right, or did the lady?

15 The more we think about the question, the harder it is to answer. Don't think about what you would do, but consider what the hot-blooded, semi-barbaric princess would do. She knew she would lose her lover, so who should have him?

16 Before the trial, the princess spent many sleepless nights. She would wake up screaming, imagining her lover being devoured by the tiger. However, even more frequently, she imagined her lover at the other door. She saw him rush to meet that woman, joyful that he would have a new life with such a beautiful lady. During those dreams, the princess would burn with agony as she saw the triumph in the eyes of the woman. She would cry out as she imagined the happy couple getting married in front of a priest. In agony, she thought about the couple walking away on a path of flowers.

17 Would it be better for him to die at once and wait for the princess in the blessed regions of eternity? Yet there was that awful tiger, the blood, and the terrifying screams.

18 The princess deliberated for many days and nights before the trial. She knew what she would do. Without hesitation, she moved her hand to indicate the door on the right.

19 The question of what decision the princess made is not easy to answer. So I leave it up to all of you: Who came out of the opened door—the lady or the tiger?

(1223 words)

COMPREHENSION

9 The princess had two different dreams. What did she imagine?

She saw her lover being devoured by the tiger.

She also imagined him rushing to meet the beautiful woman.

She saw the triumph in the eyes of the other woman.

She imagined the happy couple being married by the priest and walking away on a path of flowers.

10 Frank Stockton originally wrote this story to tell at a party. Why did he leave it with no ending?

He wanted people to discuss the story and create their own ending.

READING GROUP ACTIVITY

Work with a team of at least six students. Then choose a partner from your team. Each pair of students must choose one of the following activities. Work with your partner to complete your activity.

Group 1: Questions

With your partner, create eight questions about the story. Do not copy any of the questions listed above. Then divide a piece of paper into eight pieces. Write your questions on one side of the paper and the answers on the other side. Create questions with a variety of question words.

When you rejoin your teammates, show them the questions, one at a time. Your teammates must try to answer each question. Then you can turn each paper over and show the answers.

Group 2: Definitions

With your partner, choose eight to ten difficult words from the story. Then, on small pieces of paper, write the difficult words on one side and the definitions on the other side.

When you rejoin your other teammates, show them the words in sequence. Your teammates must guess what the words mean. Then you can turn each paper over to show the answers.

Group 3: Story Arc

With your partner, write ten sentences that sum up the story. Do not take sentences directly from the text; instead, create your own sentences. Put your sentences in chronological order. Cut a paper into ten parts, and write one sentence on each piece of paper.

When you join the rest of the group, the other team members must put the parts of the story in the correct order.

DISCUSSION AND WRITING

Discuss the following topics. Then choose two topics and write a paragraph about each one. Give each paragraph a title.

- In paragraph 6, the writer states, "In the kingdom, the trials in the arena were very popular." Why would such spectacles be so popular?
- Explain what advice you would give the accused man. What door should he open?
- What is the punishment for women in the kingdom? Make a guess.
- Imagine that you are the princess. What choice would you make?
- This story creates very one-dimensional characters. Write a paragraph inventing a background for one of the story's characters. Explain what happened to the character before the story began.
- Rewrite Part 3. Create a clear ending for the story.

Grammar TIP

Using *Would* and *Should*

Use ***would*** to indicate a possibility or desire. Use ***should*** to give advice. Use the base verb form after ***would*** and ***should***.

base form   base form
*I **would** choose the left door. The accused **should** not open the door.*

To learn more about modal auxiliaries, see Unit 9 in *Avenues 1: English Grammar.*

Writing a Paragraph

Generating Ideas

When you are given a writing assignment, two useful strategies to help you develop your ideas include **brainstorming** and **clustering**.

BRAINSTORMING

Create a list of ideas. Don't worry about grammar or spelling—the point is to generate ideas.

> EXAMPLE: Inexpensive ways to enjoy life
> - walk in a park
> - drive with the windows open
> - sleep in the hot sun
> - eat wild raspberries
> - make someone laugh really hard

CLUSTERING

Draw an idea in a circle. Then use connecting lines and circles to show your other ideas.

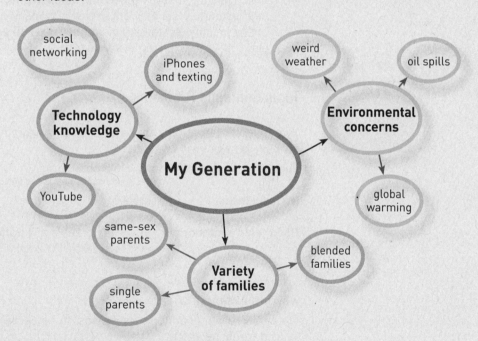

Compose It

Generate Ideas

Use brainstorming or clustering strategies. Develop ideas related to one of the following topics, or choose your own topic. (Use a separate sheet of paper.)

   Bad habits   Health   Consumer culture

Other topics: _____

The Topic Sentence

A **paragraph** contains one main idea, presented in the **topic sentence**. The other sentences in the paragraph support the main idea. Your **topic sentence** should have the following qualities.

- It is a complete sentence.
- It is the most general sentence in the paragraph.
- It expresses the **topic**.
- It contains a **main idea** that presents the focus of the paragraph.

topic   + main idea
My lab partner has many interesting qualities.

WRITING EXERCISE 1

Answers will vary.

Read the following paragraphs. Write a topic sentence for each paragraph.

1 Topic sentence: ___There are several steps you can take to reduce your water___
___consumption.___

First, take shorter showers. Five minutes is enough time to get clean. Also, only do the laundry when there is a full load. When brushing your teeth, don't leave the water running. Just turn the water on and off as needed. Finally, ask your landlord to install toilets that use very little water. Remember that water is a precious resource.

2 Topic sentence: ___Daycare has positive effects on children.___

First, children in daycare become independent. They learn to separate from their parents. Also, they are exposed to many viruses, so they develop strong immune systems. Finally, they develop social skills because they play with other children every day.

Topic Sentence Problems

Your topic sentence must make a point. It should not be vague. Do not write *My topic is …* or *I will write about …*

Vague: This is a big problem.
                        (What is a problem? The topic is unclear.)

No main idea: I will talk about bicycle riders.
                        (What is the main point? This says nothing relevant about the topic.)

Good topic sentence: Bicycle riders break many traffic laws.
                        (The topic is clear and there is a main idea.)

WRITING EXERCISE 2

Answers will vary. Possible answers are indicated.

Write "OK" under good topic sentences. If the sentence is vague, incomplete, or lacks a focus, rewrite it.

1 I will write about my lab partner.

___(No main idea) My lab partner is a hard-working and fun person.___

2 Credit cards are dangerous for some people.

___OK___

3 I will write about stress.

(No main idea) Many students have too much stress in their lives.

4 Singing is good for the health.

OK

5 This is my dream vacation.

(Vague) My dream vacation is to visit Mexico.

Compose It	**Write Topic Sentences**

You can suggest your own topics in the Compose It sections.

Write a topic sentence for two of the following topics. You can also choose your own topics. Remember to first narrow your topic down to give it a more specific focus.

Bad habits   Health   Consumer culture

Other topics: _____

EXAMPLE: *Topic:* ___Work___   *Specific topic:* ___Tipping of service workers___

Topic sentence: ___The rules about tipping service workers are___
not clear.

1. Topic: _____   Specific topic: _____

Topic sentence: _____

_____

2. Topic: _____   Specific topic: _____

Topic sentence: _____

_____

The Supporting Ideas

When you finish writing the topic sentence, you must think of specific evidence that supports it. You can include facts, anecdotes, examples, and reasons.

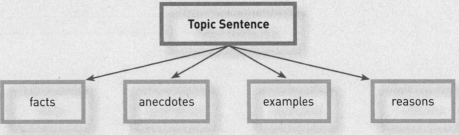

WRITING EXERCISE 3

Write three supporting ideas for each of the following topic sentences.

EXAMPLE: I made several spending mistakes.

1. ___I bought a shirt that I never wear.___

2. ___I paid too much for my car.___

3. ___I bought a new cellphone, but it is not as good as my old phone.___

1 My class partner is very compatible with me.

1. _____
   _____

2. _____
   _____

3. _____
   _____

2 We are very lucky to live in this country.

1. _____
   _____

2. _____
   _____

3. _____
   _____

3 A good life includes the following elements.

1. _____
   _____

2. _____
   _____

3. _____
   _____

Compose It

You can assign your own topics here. More detailed writing topics appear at the end of each skills chapter.

Write a Stand-Alone Paragraph

Compose a paragraph on one of the following topics or choose your own topic. Ensure that your paragraph contains a topic sentence and supporting facts and examples. Also, ensure that it is coherent. Every sentence should relate to the topic sentence.

Bad habits   Health   Consumer culture

Other topics: _____

Writing an Essay

An **essay** is divided into three parts: an **introduction**, a **body**, and a **conclusion**. Look at the following example to see how different types of paragraphs form an essay.

Learning about Finances

The **introduction** begins with general statements about the topics.

Everyone needs to learn about money. We need money to pay for food and clothing. We also need money for shelter. But if we make mistakes with our finances, this can cause a long-term disaster. **Everyone should learn to use money responsibly.**

The **thesis statement** tells the reader what the essay is about.

Each **body paragraph** begins with a **topic sentence**.

Parents need to teach children about saving. During childhood, children can develop good spending habits. For example, when I was a child, I did chores to earn money. When I wanted something, my mother would not just buy it for me. She told me to save. When I was eleven, I saved for almost one year because I wanted to buy a video game console. It was a great lesson.

Each **body paragraph** contains details that support the thesis statement.

Also, high schools should give courses on managing personal finances. Schools should instruct students about making a budget and using a credit card. This is important, because when we turn eighteen, credit card companies send us applications. It is easy to buy things on credit and then end up with problems. For instance, my brother is twenty-four, and he has a very large credit card bill.

The **conclusion** briefly restates the main points.

Everybody needs to learn to make a budget and save money. Disasters can always happen, such as losing a job. So learning about finances is important.

The Introduction

The **introductory paragraph** introduces the subject of your essay. It helps your reader understand why you are writing the text. The thesis statement is the last sentence in your introduction.

General information

Thesis statement

Canada is a materialistic nation. At a young age, children watch commercials about breakfast cereals and toys, and they learn to desire those items. In fact, the average child sees thousands of advertisements before the age of six. **Advertisers have too much influence in our culture.**

The Thesis Statement

The **thesis statement** is a sentence that expresses the main idea of an essay. Look at the following thesis statements.

> Some video games promote violence.

> To have a good life, we need strong relationships and an interesting job.

The **thesis statement** explains what the essay is about. A **topic sentence** explains what a paragraph is about. Each topic sentence supports the thesis statement.

Thesis statement	Celebrations help people in several ways.

Topic sentence 1	Topic sentence 2
When people enter a new life stage, a celebration brings families together.	Religious holidays and festivals help families feel like part of the community.

THESIS STATEMENT CHECKLIST

A thesis statement must have the following qualities.

- **It is a complete statement.** Your thesis should have a subject and a verb and express a complete idea.

  Incomplete: The best things about travelling.

  Thesis: Travelling teaches us about other cultures.

- **It expresses a clear topic and a main idea.** Ensure that your thesis statement expresses a point of view or attitude. Avoid phrases such as *My topic is* and *I will write about.*

  Vague: I had a big problem.
  (The topic is unclear.)

  No main idea: I will discuss my car accident.
  (This sentence has no focus and says nothing relevant about the topic.)

  Thesis: My car accident changed my life.

WRITING EXERCISE 1

Examine each of the following statements. If it is a good thesis statement, write TS on the line provided. If it is not a good thesis statement, then identify the problem. Write *incomplete*, *vague*, or *no main idea* on the line.

EXAMPLE: I will talk about driving.   No main idea

People should not drink and drive.   TS

1. The high cost of student housing.   Incomplete

2. In this paper, I will discuss my job.   No main idea

3. Some musicians are very bad role models.   TS

4. The problems with tattoos.   Incomplete

5. This changed my life.   Vague

6. Art courses teach students important skills.   TS

WRITING EXERCISE 2

Write a thesis statement for each of the following groups of supporting ideas. Ensure that your thesis statement is complete and expresses a clear topic and main idea.

Answers will vary. Possible answers are indicated.

EXAMPLE: Thesis: _____When you buy a car, make an informed decision._____

   a. Ask family members what type of car would be most useful.

   b. Determine how much money you can afford to pay for the car.

   c. Do research on the Internet about the specific types of cars that you are interested in.

1 Thesis: _____The local park is becoming a dangerous place._____

   a. The park is often filled with aggressive dogs.

   b. Also, in the park, there are broken bottles in children's play areas.

   c. Furthermore, during the evenings, gangs meet in the park, and there are often fights.

2 Thesis: _____There are several reasons why I never became a smoker._____

   a. First, I do not smoke because I grew up in a household full of smokers, and I hated the smell of cigarettes.

   b. Also, my grandmother died of lung cancer.

   c. Finally, my best friends don't smoke, so I never felt pressure to develop the habit.

Compose It

Write Thesis Statements

Ask students to work in pairs and to generate thesis statements.

Write thesis statements for two of the following topics, or choose your own topics. Remember to narrow each topic and to give it a specific focus.

   Nature   Celebrations   Travel   Adolescence

Other topics: _____

Introduction Styles

You can introduce your essay in several ways.

· **General background**: You can write a few general sentences about the topic.

· **Historical background**: You can give some historical information about the topic.

· **Anecdotal**: You can tell a true story about something that happened. Your story should relate to the topic.

You end your introduction with the thesis statement, which expresses the main point of the essay.

WRITING EXERCISE 3

In the following introductions, the thesis statement is in bold. Decide what introduction style is used in each paragraph.

1 In the past, skateboards were not safe. The wheels were hard, and skateboarders had many accidents. In 1960, skateboarding became so dangerous that the sport lost popularity. But new inventions, such as rubber wheels and better bearings, made skateboarding a safer activity. **Skateboarding is an exciting and important sport.**

   Style: a. General   (b.) Historical   c. Anecdotal

2 There are many ways to exercise. Every city has gyms and other sporting clubs. Information about healthy food is also easy to find. Food labels tell consumers about the sugar and salt in foods. **Some simple steps can help you to improve your health.**

Style: (a.) General   b. Historical   c. Anecdotal

3 Justin Bieber's mother put one of his songs on YouTube. Six months later, American music companies contacted the young boy from Ontario. Soon, he became an international star. **YouTube is having a large impact on the entertainment industry.**

Style: a. General   b. Historical   (c.) Anecdotal

Compose It — Write an Introduction

Write an introduction for an essay on one of the following topics, or choose your own topic. End your introduction with a clear thesis statement.

   Nature   Celebrations   Travel   Adolescence

Other topics: _____

The Supporting Ideas

In an essay, each body paragraph provides supporting evidence for the thesis statement.

> **Introduction**
> The **thesis statement** identifies the main idea of the essay.

> **Body paragraphs**
> The **topic sentence** identifies the main idea in each supporting paragraph.
>
> Facts — Anecdotes — Relevant quotations

WRITING EXERCISE 4

Ask students to read the paragraphs with a partner. They can brainstorm topic sentences together.

Read the following essay and do the following:
- First, underline the thesis statement.
- Then write a topic sentence at the beginning of each body paragraph. The topic sentence should sum up the main point of the paragraph in an interesting way.

Introduction

Many countries have English-speaking populations. The United Kingdom, Australia, New Zealand, and Scotland are just some of the places where English is the first language. Around the world, more than one billion people speak English as a second language. <u>You should learn English for two main reasons.</u>

Support 1

Topic sentence: ___First, English makes travelling easier.___

_____

In many countries, people communicate with tourists in English. For example, in Mexico City, most hotel employees speak English. When I travelled to Greece and Germany, I used my English in restaurants and on trains. Even in China, people in the tourism industry learn to communicate in English.

Support 2

Topic sentence: _Also, English is important for work._

Many companies have offices across Canada and the United States. Employees may need to communicate with people in other offices. Also, even when a company is French or Spanish, the customers may speak English. For example, Sasha Jasyk works at a software design company in Quebec City. Sasha speaks French with his co-workers, but he must often speak English with American clients. Therefore, the ability to speak English properly can improve your position in a company, and it can make you a more valuable employee.

Conclusion

When you have a chance to learn English, take it seriously. Your English ability can help you in your travels and your career.

Compose It   List Supporting Ideas

Choose one of your thesis statements from the Compose It section on page 133 and then, on a separate sheet of paper, brainstorm a list of supporting ideas for your topic.

EXAMPLE: Thesis: People travel for several reasons.
Supporting ideas: – too much stress at work
– learn about cultures
– eat exotic foods
– try new sports and activities
– practise another language

The Conclusion

You can conclude your essay by rephrasing your main points. Then you can end with a suggestion or a prediction. The following conclusion ends an essay about cellphone etiquette.

Remind the reader of your main points.

End with a prediction or suggestion.

In conclusion, cellphone users do not show enough respect to the people around them. Their cellphone rings are annoying. They answer their phones in movie theatres and classrooms. Parents should teach their children about cellphone etiquette.

Read the next paragraphs and follow these steps.

- Highlight the topic sentences in body paragraphs 1 and 2. (Look for a sentence that expresses the main idea of each paragraph.)
- Then write an introduction. You can begin with an anecdote, historical information, or general information. End your introduction with a thesis statement.
- Finally, create a short conclusion.

Introduction: _____

_____

_____

_____

_____

_____

Body paragraph 1: First, students can save money when they live at home. Instead of working to pay for rent and food, students can concentrate on their studies. They won't accumulate debts. For instance, I live with my parents, and I have savings in the bank. When I finish college, I won't have any debts. My friends Gabriel and Antonio moved out of home to go to college, and they are always broke. On weekends, they rarely want to go out because they don't have enough money.

Body paragraph 2: Second, students who live at home do not have as many distractions as students who live in an apartment or dormitory. In college residences, there are often parties. People in other apartments make a lot of noise and listen to loud music. It is hard to concentrate on homework and on projects. For example, my two best friends got an apartment together. They never sleep during weekends, and now Gabriel is failing his college courses. So it is better to live at home.

Conclusion: _____

_____

_____

_____

_____

The Essay Plan

A plan is a visual map that shows the essay's main and supporting ideas. It also includes details for each supporting idea.

Thesis statement: People travel for two main reasons.

1. **Topic sentence:** They need to get away and relax.

   Support: Maybe they have too much stress at work.
      Details: My parents work very long hours and they need a break.
   Support: They want to spend time with the family.
      Details: Our family went to the lake.

You might ask students to discuss what the essay is about. Then they can write their introductions with a partner. They should highlight the thesis statement.

Ask students to work in teams and create an essay plan. They can argue the opposite point of view to the one expressed in Exercise 5. The essay topic can be "College students should not live at home."

2. **Topic sentence:** They want to learn about other cultures.

    Support: They can practise a new language.

        Details: When we went to Cancun, we practised Spanish.

    Support: They can eat new types of food.

        Details: We loved the mole, tortillas, and other treats in Mexico.

Concluding suggestion: Everybody should travel to different places.

Compose It | Create an Essay Plan

You can assign your own writing topics here. More guided writing topics appear at the end of each skills chapter.

Create an essay plan. Your teacher will give you a topic, or you can develop one of the topics from the Compose It section on page 134.

Introduction

Thesis statement: _____

_____

Body paragraph 1

Topic sentence: _____

_____

Support: _____

_____

  Details: _____

_____

Support: _____

_____

  Details: _____

_____

Body paragraph 2

Topic sentence: _____

_____

Support: _____

_____

  Details: _____

_____

Support: _____

_____

  Details: _____

_____

Conclusion

(Think of a final suggestion or prediction.) _____

_____

Revising and Editing

Revise for Correct Vocabulary

USING A DICTIONARY

Use a dictionary to ensure that your words are varied and correctly spelled.

1 Check your dictionary's features. Often, the preface contains explanations about various symbols and abbreviations. Many dual-language dictionaries contain lists of irregular verbs. See what your dictionary has to offer.

2 When you write a word in your paragraph or essay, ensure that you use the correct part of speech!

Incorrect: I hope to become a <u>veterinary</u>.
(*Veterinary* is an adjective.)

Correct: I hope to become a **veterinarian**.
(*Veterinarian* is a noun.)

WRITING EXERCISE 1

In each sentence, the underlined word contains a mistake. Look for spelling mistakes or incorrect word forms. Use a dictionary and write the correct words in the blanks. You can use an online dictionary.

EXAMPLE: We <u>past</u> many summers at the beach.   <u>passed</u>

1 In the past, people had strange <u>believes</u> about ghosts.   <u>beliefs</u>

2 During the comedy festival, I had <u>funny</u>.   <u>fun</u>

3 As a child, I was sometimes <u>scary</u> of the dark.   <u>scared</u>

4 Jason is a big <u>spending</u>. He buys everything that he wants.   <u>spender</u>

5 For <u>exemple</u>, he buys the most expensive cellphone.   <u>example</u>

6 In many <u>contries</u>, people have celebrations.   <u>countries</u>

Revise for Adequate Support

In a paragraph, support your ideas with adequate examples. You can state facts or give examples from your life or from the lives of people you know. The following paragraph needs specific examples to make it more complete.

Paragraph without adequate support:

Countries have national holidays and celebrations for many reasons. Sometimes, the holiday marks a political or historical event. Many celebrations also have a religious component. Finally, certain celebrations are fun or romantic.

WRITING EXERCISE 2

Answers will vary.

Add details and specific examples to make the sample paragraph more complete and interesting.

Countries have national holidays and celebrations for many reasons. Sometimes, the holiday marks a political or historical event. _____

_____

Many celebrations also have a religious component. _____

_____

Finally, certain celebrations are fun or romantic. _____

_____

_____

Revise for Coherence

Your writing should have coherence. In other words, it should be easy to understand. Connections between ideas should be logical. You can use different words and expressions to help the reader follow the logic of a text.

Coordinators connect ideas inside sentences. Common coordinators are *and*, *but*, *or*, and *so*.

> I love the winter, **but** I don't like driving in the snow.

Subordinators join a secondary idea to a main idea inside a sentence. Some common subordinators are *although*, *after*, *because*, *before*, *if*, *unless*, and *until*.

> I love the winter **although** I hate cleaning the snow off my car.

Transitional words or phrases connect sentences and paragraphs. Common transitional words are *first*, *then*, *however*, *therefore*, *of course*, and *in conclusion*.

> **First,** some people drive too fast.

WRITING EXERCISE 3

The examples listed below are words and expressions that are used to connect ideas. They illustrate different functions. Write a definition or translation beside any words that you do not understand.

Chronology (time)	first*	_____	next	_____
	second*	_____	suddenly	_____
	third*	_____	then	_____
	after that	_____	finally	_____
Addition	additionally	_____	furthermore	_____
	also	_____	as well	_____
Example	for example	_____	for instance	_____
Emphasis	above all	_____	in fact	_____
	clearly	_____	of course	_____
Contrast	although	_____	however	_____
	but	_____	or	_____
	on the other hand	_____	on the contrary	_____
Summary	to conclude	_____	therefore	_____
	in short	_____	in conclusion	_____

*Do not write *firstly*, *secondly*, or *thirdly*, etc. It is preferable to write *first*, *second*, and *third*, etc.

Read the following paragraphs. Underline the most appropriate transitional expression.

Most people think about their physical health. [1](<u>However</u> / Furthermore), they do not consider their emotional health. Levels of stress and depression are increasing. [2](<u>In fact</u> / Suddenly), in a recent survey, 25 percent of the respondents reported feeling anxious and tense. A certain amount of stress is normal, and even positive. Stress can push us to create and explore. Excessive stress, [3](<u>on the other hand</u> / therefore), can cause severe health problems. Headaches, backaches, and nausea are connected to stress. [4](<u>Furthermore</u> / On the contrary), high blood pressure and heart disease may also be caused by excessive stress. [5](<u>Therefore</u> / Although), people should take actions to decrease their stress.

[6](Unless / <u>Although</u>) it is impossible to completely eliminate stress, there are some strategies that can reduce it. First, eat healthy meals and exercise. [7](<u>Additionally</u> / Because), take some time each day for uninterrupted relaxation. Meditate, listen to music, or just rest on the sofa. [8](However / <u>In conclusion</u>), take care of your mind and your body.

For more practice revising and editing writing samples, view the Revising and Editing sections at the end of chapters 1 to 7.

Oral Presentations

Here are some points to remember when you make an oral presentation.

Planning Your Presentation

- **Structure your presentation.** Make your introduction appealing. Use facts or examples to support your main points. Make sure you include a conclusion.
- **Practise.** Plan your presentation and recite it in front of a mirror several times. Your teacher will not be impressed if you pause frequently to think of something to say, or if you constantly search through your notes.
- **Do not memorize your presentation.** Simply rattling off a memorized text will make you sound unnatural. It is better to speak to the audience and refer to your notes occasionally.
- **Time yourself.** Ensure that your oral presentation respects the specified time limit.
- **Use cue cards.** Write down only key words and phrases on your cards. If you copy out your entire presentation on cue cards, you could end up getting confused and losing your place. Look at the example provided.

Presentation Text

During my childhood, my parents gave me an allowance of $5 per week. I saved my money when I wanted to buy something, such as a video game. If I needed extra money for large items, I had to earn it by doing chores. I learned to save and be responsible.

Cue Card
allowance
$5 / week
video game
chores
save
responsible

Giving Your Presentation

- Look at your entire audience, not just the teacher.
- Do not read. However, you can use cue cards to prompt yourself during the presentation.
- When the assignment requires it, bring in visual or audio supports. These can help make your presentation more interesting.

Names and Titles

What is your middle name? Do you have a nickname? Read the following definitions of names. Then answer the questions that follow.

Names

First name	• Given name	Example: *Robert*
Last name / Surname	• Family name	Example: *Bowland*
Maiden name	• Married woman's original family name	
Middle name	• Name that falls between the first and last name	
	Example: *Robert Andrew Bowland*	
Nickname	• Shortened (familiar) form of a first name	
	Example: *"Bob"* is short for *Robert*.	

Titles

Mr.	• Title before a man's name	Example: *Mr. Raoul Perez*
Miss	• Title before a single woman's nam	Example: *Miss Lucy Ru*
Mrs.	• Title before a married woman's name	Example: *Mrs. Ellen Roe*
Ms.	• A woman's title regardless of marital status	Example: *Ms. Bella Smith*
Dr.	• Short form for "doctor"	Example: *Dr. Ramon Cruz*
Prof.	• Short form for "professor"	Example: *Prof. Martin Chin*

Marital Status

Single	• Not married
Married	• Legally united
Widowed	• Having lost a spouse (husband or wife) through death
Living common law	• Living as a couple but not married
Separated	• Living apart from a husband, wife, or domestic partner
Divorced	• No longer legally married

VOCABULARY EXERCISE

Elizabeth Anne Roland is a young woman. Her family and friends call her Lizzy. Last summer, she married a doctor named Richard Eric Blain.

1. What is the woman's first name? _____Elizabeth_____

2. What is her maiden name? _____Roland_____

3. What is her nickname? _____Lizzy_____

4. What is her middle name? _____Anne_____

5. What two titles can Elizabeth use?
   a. Mr.   (b.) Mrs.   c. Miss   (d.) Ms.

6. What is Richard's surname? _____Blain_____

7. What two titles can Richard use?
   (a.) Mr.   b. Mrs.   (c.) Dr.   d. Ms.

Dates and Numbers

Days of the Week

Monday   Tuesday   Wednesday   Thursday   Friday   Saturday   Sunday

Days of the week always begin with a capital letter. (*I go to the gym every Friday.*)

The most commonly confused weekdays are Tuesday and Thursday. To help you remember, Tuesday is the second (number "two") day of the week.

Months

January	February	March	April	May	June
July	August	September	October	November	December

Months always begin with a capital letter. (*I was born in January.*)

Seasons

spring   summer   fall   winter

Seasons always begin with a lower-case letter. (*I go camping every summer.*)

Dates

When you say a date, write *on* + MONTH + DAY.

The test is **on March 21st**. My birthday is **on January 3rd**.

In English, there are cardinal and ordinal numbers. Examine the differences between them.

Cardinal Numbers

1 – one	5 – five	9 – nine	13 – thirteen	17 – seventeen
2 – two	6 – six	10 – ten	14 – fourteen	18 – eighteen
3 – three	7 – seven	11 – eleven	15 – fifteen	19 – nineteen
4 – four	8 – eight	12 – twelve	16 – sixteen	20 – twenty

100 – one hundred   1000 – one thousand   1,000,000 – one million

Notice the difference between numbers that end in "teen" and "ty."

13 – thirteen   14 – fourteen   30 – thirty   40 – forty

Ordinal numbers can have different endings.

The following numbers end with the "st" sound, EXAMPLE: 1st – first.

1st, 21st, 31st, 41st, 51st, 61st, 71st, 81st, 91st

The following numbers end with the "nd" sound, EXAMPLE: 2nd – second.

2nd, 22nd, 32nd, 42nd, 52nd, 62nd, 72nd, 82nd, 92nd

The following numbers end with the "rd" sound, EXAMPLE: 3rd – third.

3rd, 23rd, 33rd, 43rd, 53rd, 63rd, 73rd, 83rd, 93rd

All other numbers end with the "th" sound, EXAMPLE: 4th – fourth.

4th, 5th, 6th, 7th, 8th, 9th, 10th, 11th, 12th, 13th, 14th, 15th, 16th, 17th, 18th, 19th, 20th

Pronunciation

Pronunciation Rules

Review the pronunciation rules. Practice exercises appear in the chapters indicated. You can also visit the Companion Website to practise your pronunciation.

Present Tense: Third-Person Singular Verb   (Chapter 2)

Rules	Sounds	Examples		
Most third-person singular verbs end in an s or z sound.	s	works	hits	eats
	z	learns	goes	says
Add –es to a verb ending in –s, –ch, –sh, –x, or –z. Pronounce the final –es as a separate syllable.	iz	touches	reaches	fixes
		watches	relaxes	places

Past Tense: Regular Verbs   (Chapter 4)

Rules	Sounds	Examples		
When the verb ends in –s, –k, –f, –x, –ch, and –sh, the final –ed is pronounced as t.	t	asked	watched	hoped
		kissed	wished	touched
When the verb ends in –t or –d, the final –ed is pronounced as a separate syllable.	id	wanted	added	counted
		related	folded	waited
For all other regular verbs, the final –ed is pronounced as d. Example: filled	d	lived	aged	moved
		killed	cured	played

Past Tense: Irregular Verbs   (Chapter 4)

Rule	Sound	Examples		
When the verb ends in –ought or –aught, pronounce the final letters as ot.	ot	bought	taught	caught
		fought	brought	thought

Th   (Chapter 6)

Rule	Sound	Examples		
To pronounce th, push your tongue between your teeth and blow gently.	th	think	three	theatre
		death	moth	breath

...

Rules	Silent Letters	Examples		
Gn: For most words, when *g* is followed by *n*, the *g* is silent.	**g**	si**g**n de**s**ign	forei**g**n resi**g**n	beni**g**n Exception: signature
Mb: When *m* is followed by *b*, the *b* is silent.	**b**	com**b** clim**b**	dum**b** plum**b**er	thum**b**
Kn: When *k* is followed by *n*, the *k* is silent.	**k**	**k**now **k**nee	**k**new **k**nit	**k**not **k**nife
L: Do not pronounce *l* in some common words.	**l**	shou**l**d ca**l**m	wou**l**d ta**l**k	cou**l**d wa**l**k
T: Do not pronounce *t* in some common words.	**t**	lis**t**en Chris**t**mas	whis**t**le fas**t**en	of**t**en cas**t**le
W: Do not pronounce *w* in some common words.	**w**	**w**rite	**w**rong	**w**ho
Gh: In some words, the *gh* is silent. (Note that in some words such as *laugh* and *cough*, *gh* sounds like *f*.)	**gh**	thou**gh**t li**gh**t	bou**gh**t thou**gh**	dau**gh**ter wei**gh**

Pronunciation Help with Online Dictionaries

Many dictionaries are available online. On *dictionary.reference.com*, the stressed syllable is indicated in bold. By clicking on the loudspeaker, you can hear the word being pronounced. (Note that *dictionary.reference.com* also has a "Thesaurus" tab.)

co·op·er·a·tion   ◄)) [koh-op-*uh*-**rey**-sh*uh*n]

From *dictionary.reference.com*

PRONUNCIATION EXERCISE

Use a regular or online dictionary to determine which syllable is accented in each word. Underline the accented syllable.

EXAMPLE: re**cep**tionist

1 la**bor**atory
2 **sec**retary
3 **eq**uitable
4 in**vent**
5 **in**ventory
6 **hap**pening
7 be**gin**ning
8 **med**icine
9 **nav**igate
10 navi**ga**tion

11 psy**chi**atrist
12 co**op**erate
13 fil**tra**tion
14 **mo**tivate
15 moti**va**tion
16 **of**fered
17 pre**fer**red
18 **hap**pened
19 **op**erate
20 ope**ra**tion

Spelling Log

Every time you misspell a word, record both the mistake and the correction in your spelling log. Then, before you hand in a writing assignment, consult the list of misspelled words. The goal is to stop repeating the same spelling errors.

Incorrect	Correct
realy	*really really really*
whit	*with with with*

Vocabulary Log

When you learn a new word, write the word and meaning on the lines provided. Also write a short sentence to show how the word is used.

Vocabulary Term	Meaning	Example
poisonous	toxic	The mushroom is poisonous.

Index

Photo Credits

© **Alamy**
p. 54 © AF archive. p. 79 © John Seagle. p. 93 © Les Breault. p. 96 © Andrew McConnell. p. 112 © ClassicStock. p. 114 top: © Radka Linkova; bottom: © S.I.N. p. 115 © Images.com. p. 116 © Pictorial Press Ltd. p. 117 top: © Interfoto.

© **Big Break Enterprises Inc.:** p. 39.

© **Bigstock**
p. 18 top left-centre: © Harveys Art; top centre: © Tupungato; bottom centre: © Njari. p. 60 bottom: © Cynoclub; p. 62 right: © Vibe Photography. p. 75 right centre: © Forgiss. p. 90 © Vtupinamba. p. 106 right: © McIninch. p. 117 bottom: C: © Vanell. p. 118 top: A: © Dougbraphael.

© **Canadian Broadcasting Corporation:** p. 46.

© **Cattani, Derek:** p. 63.

© **CP Images**
p. 103 © Tsvangirayi Mukwazhi. p. 107 © Richard Hartog, File.

© **Gaetz, Lynne:** pp. 105, 122.

© **iStockphoto**
pp. 1, 16 © Uygar Ozel. p. 10 © ARENA Creative. p. 11 © Ryan K.C. Wong. p. 12 © Chris Schmidt. p. 18 top right-centre: © Mark Evans; top right: © Ragsac; bottom left-centre: © Timurock. p. 23 top left: © Ethan Myerson; bottom right: © brett lamb. p. 28 © Catherine Yeulet. p. 35 © YinYang. p. 42 © Alex Slobodkin. p. 44 © tillsonburg. p. 72 top right: © Jaap2. p. 80 © Emmanuel Hidalgo. p. 91 © Alena Yakusheva. p. 117 bottom: A: © nicoolay. p. 118 top: C: © Hulton Archive; bottom: A: © Renee Keith. p. 123 right: © mason01.

© **Meese, Stephen:** p. 64.

© **Pelaez, Rebeka:** p. 117 bottom: B.

© **Shutterstock**
p. 2 left: © Klaus-Peter Adler; centre: © Alena Ozerova; right: © Josh Resnick. p. 3 © Stephen Coburn. p. 4 © Baloncici. p. 6 © Edita Pawlowska. p. 11 right: © Aleksandr Markin. p. 14 © Losevski Pavel. pp. 17, 33 © Jackiso. p. 18 top left: Tatiana Popova; bottom right-centre: © Boguslaw Mazur; bottom right: © Lana K. p. 23 top centre: © Maksym Bondarchuk; top right: © Joe Belanger; bottom left: © Digital Genetics; bottom centre: © Ann Baldwin. p. 25 © Bruce Rolff. p. 31 © Tadija. pp. 34, 51 © RTimages. p. 37 © iQoncept. p. 40 © i. Quintanilla. p. 45 © James Steidl. pp. 52, 68 © 2009fotofriends. p. 53 A: © RTimages; B: © Torsten Lorenz; C: © Lars Kastilan; D: © Travel Bug. p. 57 © Tyler Olson. p. 59 left: © Four Oaks; left centre: © Galina Barskaya; right centre: © R. Gino Santa Maria; right: © Chas. p. 60 top left: © Nito; top left-centre: © Bioraven; top right-centre (n.c.); top right: © Eric Isselée. p. 62 left: © Sam D'Cruz. pp. 69, 87 © Tyler Olson. p. 70 left: © Helen & Vlad Filatov; centre: © Ev Thomas; right: © Merlindo. p. 71 © Nattika. p. 72 left: © Krugloff; bottom right: © Adam36. p. 73 top: © Angela Hawkey; bottom: © Kurhan. p. 74 right: © Constructer; top left: © J. Helgason; bottom left: © Tomo. p. 75 left: © Ruslan Semichev; left centre: © Juriah Mosin; right: © Scott L. Williams. p. 82 © Juan David Ferrando. p. 83 © Roger De Marfa. p. 84 © Tipograffias. p. 88, 104 © Morgan DDL. p. 92 top: © Russ Spivey; bottom: © Neo Edmund. p. 99 © Grafica. p. 106 left: © Susan Law Cain; centre: © Elena Ray. p. 109 © Suzanne Tucker. p. 118 top: B: © Mudassar Ahmed Dar; bottom: B: © Iurii Konoval; C: © Jiri Hera. p. 123 left: © Dimitriv Shironosov. p. 124 left: © Gretasplace; right: © Styve Reineck.